GREAT BRANDING
IDEAS

Sarah McCartney

 Marshall Cavendish
Business

First published in 2012 by Marshall Cavendish Business
An imprint of Marshall Cavendish International
PO Box 65829
London EC1P 1NY
info@marshallcavendish.co.uk
and
1 New Industrial Road, Singapore 536196
genrefsales@sg.marshallcavendish.com
www.marshallcavendish.com/genref

Other Marshall Cavendish offices: Marshall Cavendish International (Asia) Private Limited, 1 New Industrial Road, Singapore 536196 • Marshall Cavendish Corporation. 99 White Plains Road, Tarrytown NY 10591-9001, USA • Marshall Cavendish International (Thailand) Co Ltd. 253 Asoke, 12th Flr, Sukhumvit 21 Road, Klongtoey Nua, Wattana, Bangkok 10110, Thailand • Marshall Cavendish (Malaysia) Sdn Bhd, Times Subang, Lot 46, Subang Hi-Tech Industrial Park, Batu Tiga, 40000 Shah Alam, Selangor Darul Ehsan, Malaysia

Marshall Cavendish is a trademark of Times Publishing Limited

A CIP record for this book is available from the British Library

ISBN 978-981-4351-21-8

Printed and bound in Great Britain by
TJ International Limited, Padstow, Cornwall

CONTENTS

About the Author

For all the things I've picked up about brands along the way, I'd like to thank colleagues at D'Arcy McManus & Masius and the Guardian and Observer newspapers, and clients past and present.

I'd like to say thankyou (which is one word, despite spellchecker's determination to break it into two) to the people who make me think hard, including Mary Linehan (PR goddess), Stephen Zades, Nick Randell, Ben Afia and the board of 26.

Particular thanks to Martin Liu at Marshall Cavendish who listens to my ideas, quite often commissions them, then lets me get on and write them.

INTRODUCTION

Whether you run a multinational or a social enterprise, a charity or a one-man-band, you have a brand.

Branding is all about deciding where you stand, and what makes you different from the others, then showing and telling the difference as clearly as you can to make you brand stand out.

Everything that a brand is and does forms part of its identity.

Building a brand's identity makes it more recognisable, familiar and reassuring—as long as you get it right. If it's all going well, then people are more likely to chose your brand, use it and tell their friends about it.

Your branding is working when you've got people saying, "Yes, I know them. They're the people who …

"… have the big blue building in the centre of town."

"… make those delicious biscuits."

"… sponsor our football team."

"… designed my favourite jacket."

What's important is that people remember the good things about your brand, come back to it or recommend it to people they know, and don't get you mixed up with someone else.

In this book, there are 100 branding ideas; some are about brand strategy and some about specific actions you could take. Use them to give you direction, or to help evaluate the branding you're already doing. You can read it from start to finish, or you can also pick a page at random.

All the stories are here to make a point, not just as anecdotes.

I use them to shed light on a situation that might arise again, and which you might approach differently for your own brand.

They won't all be relevant to you right now but some of them will, and I do hope they give you something new to think about, debate and adapt for your own use.

Brands are people's and organisations' intellectual property, so you'll have to adapt some of the examples I've written about before you can apply a similar idea to your own organisation. But that's where innovation and creativity come in; define what you can and can't do, and this will help you to invent a your own solution to a particular problem.

PS

Point 101: Tell the truth. In these days of social media and the speed that news can travel around the Internet, if you try to put a glossy face on a grubby reality, you'll get found out. The best branding comes from building a great organisation, then letting people know all about it.

1 KNOW WHAT A BRAND IS

People think they know what brands are, but often they don't. I've heard business people say, "Oh no, we don't really have a brand, we just run a business." Clothes shoppers will tell me, "I don't buy brands, they're too expensive. I go to the Gap, Next or Uniqlo."

A brand isn't something that's too expensive for most of us to buy—that's a luxury brand. A brand is any product or service (and occasionally an individual) that stands out from the others around it because of its positioning or its personality. All organisations are brand owners whether they like it or not, and they've a responsibility for how other people regard that brand.

The most important thing is to stand out.

The idea

A brand is much more than a logo or a name. As well as its easily defined features, like its colour and its location, it's made up of the feelings it evokes in people. Each individual will feel something different about the brand according to personal experience, and this is something a brand owner can't control.

However you should still give it your best shot. As the brand owner, it's your responsibility to influence the way people think about your brand, and you do that by taking care of each experience your customers have when they come into contact with the organisation. Dividing a brand into positioning and personality comes from an excellent academic book, Branding In Action, by Graham Hankinson and Philippa Cowking.

When they talk about positioning, they mean where your brands fit compared with all the others you compete with. Where do you fit in the price versus quality scale? And what do people use your brand for?

With personality, Hankinson & Cowking's book includes things that you definitely control, like the typeface you use your corporate colours your logo, where you're based, where people come into contact with you.

Personality is also made up of perceptions which are much more difficult to pin down. How do people see you? Are you traditional or modern? Are you safe or risky? Do people think you're really good value or cheap? Do people think your excellent quality or way too expensive, or both?

When you know what's at the heart of your brand, it can help to define what you should do next.

In practice

- Look at your brand positioning. On the price scale, where do you fit among the brands you compete with?
- Looking at "usage", what Hankinson & Cowking mean is when, where, why and how people would choose your brand rather than an alternative one. If people want a cup of coffee would they choose a different brand at home, from when they buy a takeaway or when they go with a friend for a chat. What do your customers use you for? Where you fit into the market compared with your competitors? How can you increase your chances of being the one they choose?
- As for your personality, list the words you think people would use to define your brand's identity if it were a person.

2 SOUND LIKE YOUR VALUES

When a brand first comes into being, it's often the result of much hard thinking, planning and creativity by its founder, inventor or the small team behind it. The people working close to creative centre pick up their creators' enthusiasm and passion, and everyone involved talks about the brand in the same way. They can speak the brand language.

Years go by, the company grows, the brand name is still there and people are doing their jobs. But the links to the brand's beating heart, the connections to the creative team, have weakened or faded away.

The idea

Part of business writing for brands is to work with organisations to help them articulate their brand personalities, to put their brands into words. Odd things happen to people when they start to write for a business. They believe that they've to use all the longest words they know, and jam in all the facts they've ever picked up. Sometimes, the people at the very top are often the worst culprits. They've learned the habit of writing to sound important instead of interesting.

They completely forget that someone has to read what they've written, and act on it.

This often happens within organisations whose brands have been in existence for decades, maybe centuries, and their people fall into the habit of using the same phrases that have been repeated without question for years.

Each brand's values are different. Here are some examples:

- reliable, traditional, family-run, polite
- international, technological, cutting-edge, powerful
- challenging, innovative, urban, modern
- cheap, cheerful, no-frills, friendly

You'd hope that a letter, a blog, a web copy or an internal memo would pick up on their values and sound as if it has the brand's stamp on it. Often they don't.

Telling your people what your brand values are and asking them suddenly to write in a campaigning, dedicated, purposeful and focused way is expecting the impossible. Ask a copywriter to do it and he or she probably could. Training your people to write in a style that suits your brand is the best way to go about it.

When Aviva went through the biggest rebrand in UK history (changing from Norwich Union) they ran a huge writing training programme as part of a whole became clearer and more purposeful, and sounded as if it came from individual writers, not a faceless corporation.

In practice

- First, be clear. If there is any possibility of misunderstanding what you've written, explain or rewrite.
- Always remember that there's a person at the end of your writing. Put yourself in their shoes and ask if what you're writing sounds like the brand you represent.

- Assume that people will not understand the industrial jargon that you use with your colleagues, and use everyday words wherever you can. The BBC and The Economist recommend this too in their writing style guides..

3 KNOW WHERE YOU STAND

Everyone involved in running a brand need to know where it stands in the market. With a clear picture of who you are and what you do, you can mark out your territory, clearly explain to customers what makes you different from other brands and also make the right decisions about which direction to take the organisation.

The idea

We aren't talking about mission statements. Although a mission statement is intended to distinguish you from other organisations and be something that applies only to you, usually they come out sounding dull as ditchwater and lacking emotional understanding of what it is about the brand that appeals to its customers.

We're talking about something that goes much deeper: What your organisation believes in. Without it, it's too easy to say yes to all the interesting ideas presented to you by your people and your creative agencies, or to feel that you have to respond to something new from your competitors.

Knowing who you are, what you stand for and where you're going next, you give yourself a clear picture of what's right and what's wrong for your brand.

A great example is the motorcycle company Harley-Davidson. They cut costs to complete with the Japanese motorcycle industry in the 70s and 80s. Then they paused, thought it through and redefined themselves. This is encapsulated in the film they made for their own staff, known as "Creed". You can find it on YouTube. When you watch it, even if you've never owned a motorbike, just for a moment you imagine you're riding on the open road in a warm Californian breeze.

The cosmetics company, Lush, is another organisation that has a clear understanding of where they stand in the market. They write what they believe in, "A Lush Life", on blackboards in each of their shops, on their website and in their newspaper, *The Lush Times*.

In practice

- If it's been a while since you asked yourself what makes your organisation great, and what makes it different from everyone else, take some time to think it through.
- Ask your own people and your customers what they think you stand for, and compare the results.
- Work on your statement of what you stand for until you can explain it clearly to anyone who asks.

4 STAY CONSISTENT

Once you've decided what your brand stands for, you should have a checklist to help you decide whether a new project or idea will help to take you in the direction you want your brand to go.

Even if you've never read a marketing textbook, or set foot inside a branding agency, you can probably spot when an organisation does something that just feels wrong. They've gone to the trouble of building a brand position in their market, then suddenly they do something weird that doesn't seem to fit with their usual behaviour.

In brand dialect this is known as being inconsistent with your brand identity.

To stay consistent, memorise the checklist that defines who you are, and if you find yourself straying away from it, guide yourself gently back to the right path.

The idea

At New York's Museum of Modern Art (MoMA) shop, every single item that you can buy there is a minor work of art itself. Instead of just being a place you strolled through on the way out to pick up a few souvenirs to remind you of your visit, it became a stand-alone art and design hub that people visit to buy beautiful things, independently of a trip to the museum. This was such a great idea that museums around the world have done the same thing. In the past, museum shops would offer a paltry selection of pencils and rulers, coasters and tea towels with the museum's name printed on, which you could buy to disappoint your relatives and friends. Now, museums like Baltic, the Science Museum and the National Gallery all have shops whose contents, although not quite as rare and valuable as the exhibits, are equally interesting and beautiful.

My favourite failure was a furniture shop with a small display of hand-knitted toys in one corner of the window. Someone must have thought it was a great idea, and maybe they did occasionally sell a toy, but they must have frightened off furniture customers by doing something so odd that it raised questions about their ability to make rational decisions.

In practice

- Use your brand values as a reference. When you're presented with a new idea, especially if it seems a good financial prospect, check that it's consistent with your brand values. If it isn't, you might want to decide against it.
- If you get the feeling that there's something not quite convincing about the decision you're facing, go over your brand values again. It's probably not consistent.
- Review your brand values once in a while. Times change; your customers' needs change. If you find that the new ideas presented to you always share a common inconsistency with your brand values, perhaps it's time to tweak your values to match the changing times. Once every five years ought to be about right.

5 MAKE IT CUTE

Among children–and adults who are still in touch with their inner infant–cute stuff is amazingly popular. From backpacks in the shape of penguins that look like they're hitching a ride on a child's shoulders, to teddy bear ears that motorcycle riders stick onto their crash helmets, there is a market for cuteness. In Japan, where cuteness is taken to its limits, the word that describes adorable, sweet things is *kawaii*, often heard squealed at high volume whenever Japanese girls spot something fluffy with large eyes.

The idea

Originally designed for children but with a massive adult fan base (both serious and ironic), the queen of *kawaii* is Hello Kitty. This cute kitten character who is so popular she has her own theme park, Sanrio Puroland, in a Tama New Town, Tokyo, and another in China. The large-headed, huge-eyed cat character has stormed the Far East, had her own department in Harrods and appears on hundreds of products from stickers to sugar candies.

You might imagine that cute and sophisticated wouldn't mix, but Louis Vuitton (LV) commissioned Japanese artist Takashi Murakami, who specialises in creating unusual *kawaii* characters, to decorate their normally sober brown and gold monogrammed canvas bags. Featuring smiling cherries or happy flowers, these bags flew out of the stores, in Japan and around the world. This was the brainchild of LV designer Marc Jacobs, blending two of Japan's biggest obsessions the LV logo plus cuteness.

Cuteness often works best where you're least expecting it, like a fluffy bunny tail on the back of a smartly tailored Moschino jacket. It makes people smile. While it's not to everyone's taste, and should be used sparingly by serious brands, it's a way to reach new markets.

In practice

- Make it fluffy, pink or put polka dots and a ribbon on it – those things that symbolise sweet, childish things.
- Add a smiley face.
- Make sure that it adds to your brand identity before you go along the cute route.

STEALTH BRANDING

Not everyone wants to broadcast their brand allegiance by wearing clothing and accessories that are plastered with logos. On the other hand they might not want to go completely anonymous. There are ways to send brand signals to people who know how to understand them, but which go unnoticed by those who don't.

The idea

In the 1970s Stan Smith's tennis shoes had the "Green Flash" sole, part of his branding that you could see as the wearer ran across the tennis court to make a shot. They were the must have shoe for school sports, partly because they were cool and partly because green wasn't part of regulation school uniform so you could wear the white shoes and still break the rules just slightly.

These days, it's the red flash that turns heads amongst the shoe cognoscenti. Christian Louboutin shoes have red soles. Some people know this, many don't. They're at the top end of the shoe market and make all their shoes, from skyscraping stilettos to elegant flats, with a scarlet sole, seen from behind as their wearers walk. In 1992 he wanted to add a certain something to make his shoes stand out, so he took red nail varnish and painted the soles red. Since then, he has used a lacquer to give his shoes their shiny scarlet signature.

Louboutin aimed to protect his signature red design vigorously using intellectual property law, and by educating customers in ways to spot counterfeits. Whether or not one can trademark such a distinctive feature depends on the country's intellectual property laws, and these vary from extremely tough in France, to flimsy to the point of ineffectual in part of the developing world. In 2011 he lost a crucial ruling, against Yves Saint Laurent's use of red soles in their 2011-12 collection, when the courts decided that no-one can own the colour red within the fashion industry.

There is a controversial view that even if a counterfeiter can legally copy what Christian Louboutin does, each red flash works in Louboutin's favour as each one acts as an advertisement for the genuine article. Those who buy the real thing because of the quality workmanship would never want the copies anywhere near their feet.

With Paul Smith's shoes, you can spot his trademark stripes on the soles, if you're watching carefully.

In practice

- Pick a colour or a shape or a pattern. Trademark it if you can.
- Stick with it until people start to notice it, and continue to stick with it.
- Use it somewhere no one's thought of, until now.

7 OPEN A MUSEUM

Brands which have a genuine, unbroken history can distinguish themselves from those who have adopted a traditional look, by exhibiting artefacts in their own museum. While there may not be room in every organisation's offices or shops to display their entire archive, a carefully chosen, well-designed cabinet of curiosities will give customers and staff new ways to connect with the brand.

In some countries, antiques are merely seen as second-hand things for people who can't afford new ones. Know your market. Where vintage styles and traditions are valued, tasteful display of your vintage products will add to your brand's authenticity in your customers' eyes.

The idea

Smythson of Bond Street is a great brand for many reasons. They have manufactured stationery in the UK and had a shop in London's West End since 1887. Their customers include the Queen and countless members of the British nobility. Although they are no longer a family company, they are still on Bond Street, and customers can walk through their shop to visit the little museum of stationery which they've produced for famous people through the years.

Recently, in their printed catalogues, they've used archive illustrations of their jewellery boxes, portable offices, briefcases and small leather goods from their early years. All this demonstrates their authenticity and—without ever mentioning the competition—casually dismissed their rivals as modern upstarts.

In practice

- Explore your cupboards, unpack the oldest boxes, look up your records and unveil your archives. Look for stories you can tell about your origins and your past customers.
- Show how your organisation has changed since the start, while holding on to its original values.
- Surprise customers who knew nothing about your history.

NAMING 1: GIVE YOURSELF TWO MEANINGS

Naming is a specialism within branding which can take months, and millions. Considering the amount that organisations spend on packaging, advertising and many other things that go into launching a new brand, it's understandable that they want to get the name right. Some use specialist agencies, but most companies invent their own names, some of which are excellent.

When you're naming a brand in English, you are presented with an array of potential double meanings which sometimes work for you, but can work against you. If you're naming in English, and English isn't your first language, please do check with a native speaker that you haven't mistakenly used one of our many many double meanings. Some of them can be rather rude. On the other hand, when you do it successfully you create a memorable name for yourself.

The idea

Yogamatters is a small British company started at the end of the 20th century. Unsurprisingly, their very first product was yoga mats. Given that a hatter is someone who makes or sells hats, it's reasonable to think that a matter would be someone who makes or sells mats. Everyone at Yogamatters practises yoga and many are qualified teachers; they even have their own yoga studio at their north London premises. So it's equally true to say that yoga matters to them.

They use a play on words that will make people smile in recognition. They've positioned themselves as a committed, friendly yoga organisation by combining two words in a playful and intelligent way.

There is no easy way to set about a naming project. Sometimes a name will come to you seemingly out of the blue—probably from years of thinking about brand names and collecting inspiration from all around you—but there is no guarantee that this will happen when you want it to.

In practice

- Write down all the words you can think of that apply to your organisation. Combine them in pairs, then see if something useful drops out.
- Always check that the name isn't already a registered trademark in your area of business.

NAMING 2: RENAMING YOUR BRAND

Human beings love changing things, particularly when we first encounter them. When we move into a new house we look around and say to ourselves, "We could move this. We could paint that. We could knock this wall down." Once we've been in place for a while, we stop noticing things that need changing because we've accustomed ourselves to them.

The same thing happens with brands. When we start a new project, or we're brought in to revitalise an old one, we really want to make things better, to throw out all the old stuff and start again. The question to ask is, "Will the benefits outweigh the costs?" Those costs include losing the brand loyalty that you have built over the years.

The idea

In the 1990s, the UK higher education system went through a series of change in which many higher education colleges became polytechnics, and polytechnics were upgraded to university status. Ealing College was a polytechnic for such a short space of time, the name change only merited a canvas banner hung at the front of the building before it changed again to Thames Valley University, TVU for short.

Later, TVU realised that they were the only university with a London postcode that did not mention London in their name. Many students at TVU are from from overseas, so they only realised they'd be living in London once they arrived to start their studies. Having London in the brand name, taking advantage of being part of one of the world's most vibrant cities, is an attraction. Thames Valley University were potentially missing out on recruiting students who wanted to live in London.

In May 2011, TVU became UWL, the University of West London. Not only is this a more accurate statement of their location, it has become a more attractive brand by hitching its cart to London's own identity.

It's not always a great idea to change your name, even if you think that the current one is old-fashioned. If your brand has become tarnished, associated with bad practice or poor quality, then it's definitely time to consider a change.

Or, like TVU, if your brand name does not accurately represent what you stand for, you have a case for renaming.

But if you have a widely known brand with strong customer loyalty—like the magazine *Good Housekeeping*, which is not something you'd name a magazine these days—resist the temptation to change and leave it be. Never change just for the sake of change.

Bearing in mind that once you rename your brand you will lose much of the identity you have invested in, weigh up the risks and costs of change against staying the same.

In practice

- Find out what your customers think of your brand name, and what it stands for.
- If you discover that your brand has more negative associations than positive, first explore the words you could use to change people's perceptions.

- Put together a team to explore all options, check that the trademark is free, do the costings, and test your ideas first.
- If you're still sure you need to change, go ahead.

NAMING 3: NAME YOUR COMPANY AFTER YOURSELF

One traditional way of naming a company is to call it by the name of its founder, or to name it after the place it originated from. Mars, the food company that is well-known for its chocolate bars, is named after its founder, Frank C. Mars. Renault and Mercedes Benz were named after their owners. BMW, Bayerische Motoren Werke, is named after its location of origin.

Other established brands that were named after their owners, and are still going strong, include Harrods, Selfridge's, Bloomingdale's, Macy's and John Lewis.

Now, with many brands created with the intention of going worldwide, their founders rarely use their own names but search for—or invent—words that are pronounceable and unoffensive to various cultures. Some combine the two, like Nick Dyson and his eponymous vacuum cleaners.

The idea

Paul Smith, the British designer, has built an international reputation for his clothes and accessories. His name, as I'm sure he would be the first to admit, is a very ordinary one. Smith is the most popular British surname but because of its popularity it has an innate Britishness. Paul is a straightforward, no messing, common or garden first name with no pretensions whatsoever. It suits Paul Smith the man very well.

In traditional tailoring, it's the custom to name your shop after yourself. In 1979, when Paul Smith set up shop in Nottingham, fashion brands were more likely to invent themselves a brand name. So it's almost by good fortune that Paul Smith happens to have a name which suits his brand perfectly.

In practice

- Does your own name have the same kind of brand feel to it as the market you intend to operate in? If the answer is yes, and you think your customers will be able to pronounce it, then it's definitely one of your options.
- If you're in an industry like perfumery where real names are traditionally used as brand names, and you wish to fit right in, then add yours to the list of names you're considering.
- Even if your real name is Macdonald, if you're planning to open a fast-food restaurant, you might find yourself with a legal situation on your hands. Before you choose a name, always check whether or not it's been trademarked for your market before you commit yourself.

11 NAMING 4: A BIG HINT

Modern names often encapsulate a vision of their brand identity. Companies like innocent drinks, Lush Fresh Handmade Cosmetics, One Coconut Water, Whole Foods Markets in the real world or StumbleUpon, YouSendIt and Facebook on the Internet; they all have names that give you an idea of what they do.

There's also the king of the big hint, I Can't Believe It's Not Butter.

The idea

The Body Shop was set up in Berkeley, California, in 1970 by Jane Saunders and Peggy Short. The big hint is pretty obvious; this is a shop that sells things for your body.

Before the 1970s, a body shop was a place you took your car to have the bodywork fixed, dents beaten out, chips repaired and the like. In the automotive industry, it still is. In those days, calling a cosmetics store The Body Shop was an interesting twist in the language, a brand name that borrowed an established term from another industry. Jane and Peggy got their inspiration from their building's former use; it really had been a car body shop.

There is a sequel to this particular story. The Body Shop is better known in its second incarnation. Anita Roddick visited California, went to The Body Shop and decided that it was such a great idea, she returned to the UK and set up her own version, opening her first shop in 1976. As The (Roddick) Body Shop expanded around the world, they were unable to open shops in the US as the registered trademark belonged to the original owners. In 1987, Roddick's Body Shop bought the rights to the name from Saunders and Short, who agreed to change to Body Time. So they had to start again with a new brand name with a new a big hint brand name, with a comforting bonus of a lot more funding second time around.

In practice

- Ask yourself how people would describe your new organisation, your brand or your idea. What would they really say about it? What does it do? What is it for? Write down all the answers. Your brand name could be on the list.
- Sometimes the name comes first; you have such a great idea for a brand name that you have to invent an organisation to match it. However, usually it's a case of sitting down with a pencil and paper – or standing up with a flipchart and marker pen – getting the most creative people you know into a room all together and not letting them out until they have written down all their ideas.
- Check that the name is legally available as a trademark in all the countries you intend to operate. And not only that. Also do the localisation; check that it's not offensive or culturally inappropriate in other areas. One big hint brand name from the US is for a monitor you put on your child to check that they don't stray out of the area. It was called The Little Bugger. Not appropriate in the UK.

NAMING 5: BE SHOCKING

If and only if you know that your potential customers will be attracted rather than repelled by a brand identity that shocks, you might consider taking the risk. It will almost definitely get you talked about, but it could also get you banned.

The idea

Virgin, the brand established by Sir Richard Branson, and extended in many interesting directions—some successful, some not—first appeared at Branson's and Nik Powell's small record shop in 1970, Virgin Records and Tapes, in Notting Hill . They set up their record company in 1972. Sir Richard says that they chose the name because they were all business virgins.

Now, when the brand name Virgin is mentioned, we tend to think of Branson himself. It has a meaning that has developed beyond the original sense: A pure young woman or unspoiled territory. In the 1970s, in most of the UK, virgin was not a word that you'd say out loud in polite company. And to see it written on carrier bags, shop fronts and T-shirts really was deeply shocking.

Carrier bags for 7-inch singles were branded "Virgin Single". Daring young women would stick them up on their bedroom walls next to their Genesis posters. A girl I went to school with bought herself a Virgin T-shirt, and was instructed by the local headmaster not to walk anywhere near his junior school for fear of corrupting the pupils.

Shock worked for Branson.

On the other hand, a provocative name can create trouble. BJ Cunningham and Boz Temple-Morris established the Enlightened Tobacco Company and launched their brand, Death Cigarettes in 1991. They used a skull and crossbones as their logo. They took to view that since smokers know that cigarettes can kill them, you might as well tell the truth about it.

Their approach was too uncomfortable for the mainstream cigarette manufacturers, who allegedly discouraged stockists from selling the small brand. Allegedly. The company finally closed in 1999.

You can still see the rather splendid countertop display at www.logax.com in their "Packaging & POS" section. It did get talked about, and Death was a well-known brand for a while, but in the end, it was too threatening for the market, and a little bit too honest for the competitors to bear.

In practice

- Put yourself in your customers' shoes. Consider what they might think before you go on the shocking route. What is shocking now could become the norm in future as people accept the new meaning created by the brand name— but only if the brand lasts long enough.
- Shocking with a hint of naughtiness tends to have an advantage over shocking and confrontational.

13 NAMING 6: WORDPLAY

There are some marvellous brand names in English because we can twist and turn the language to give it several meanings at the same time. You can do this in other languages, not all, and international copywriters have all told me that English is the one you can have most fun with. It can work as long as your brand is a lighthearted one. If you're a specialist in family law, a charity or a shipping company you might want to keep it straightforward.

The idea

I have a friend with a bicycle repair company called Richard's Bicycle Works. On reading his business card, lots of English speakers will say, "Richard's Bicycle Works! I should hope so, considering that he's the one who fixed it." Then they laugh at their own little joke because they think they are the first person who thought of it. (Including me.)

In Avignon in the south of France, there's a hairdresser's shop called L'Hair du Temps. This is pronounced exactly the same way as the phrase l'air du temps, which roughly means *zeitgeist* or the way we live now. It's also the name of a Nina Ricci perfume. So by making a little *jeu de mot* and altering it to L'Hair du Temps; they're showing that they speak a little English, that you can expect a moodern cut and they'll make you smile. Hairdressers do seem to be masters of the wordplay brand name. My local is Aristocuts.

Then there is our local landscape gardeners, Cutting Hedge.

This one was spotted in Los Angeles: The Merchant of Tennis.

Yes, they are a little bit jokey, but they certainly are memorable.

In practice

- Use wordplay to name a product or a service, or for your whole organisation, only if it matches your brand's positioning.
- Take a phrase and play with it until it makes people smile.
- Test it to check that other people get the joke.
- As ever, with intellectual property, check with your country's trademark registration organisation, and worldwide, to make sure that it's available and that you can use it.

14 NAMING 7: BE POETIC

As we were saying, a hundred years ago companies generally named themselves after their owners or their location. And although they might choose a snappier brand name for their products, they generally retained a practical descriptive approach. However early brand names did sometimes venture into the poetic, with elegant metaphors to summon up a vision of the ideal.

The idea

There's a delicate balance here. How can you describe what you do clearly yet add a touch of the idyllic to your brand identity?

How about Robertson's Golden Shred marmalade with its strips of orange peel, and Cadbury's Dairy Milk chocolate? They're such familiar brands in the UK that's we have almost forgotten their meanings and the feelings that they were designed to evoke when they first appeared on jars and bars in 1996 and 1905.

The current trend is to use short names, sometimes invented, that don't already mean anything, rather than aim to associate with something that already exists, just in case it has negative associations somewhere around the world.

Evocative names abound in fine perfumery, like Tauer Perfumes' L'Air du Désert Marocain. The late lamented Keep It Fluffy, by B Never Too Busy to be Beautiful, and my favourite, Let Me Play The Lion, by Les Nez.

Band names go from the ultra short—U2—to the more lyrical, like The Divine Comedy, The Imagined Village, Snow Patrol. Then there are the Canadian bands Crash Test Dummies and their friends Bare Naked Ladies (who are men with their clothes on).

Some of the most inventive names belong to bloggers: A Donkey on the Edge, If You Lived Here You Would Be Home By Now, Random Acts of Reality and 66,000 Miles Per Hour.

In practice

- The accepted wisdom these days is to keep brand names short and snappy, but if your organisation isn't the short, snappy type, go against the grain. Not everything has to sound like a new car name.

- Make evocative names memorable. If they've too many words, customers tend to remember them wrongly.

- Cass Art uses "Let's Fill This Town With Artists" on their shop fronts. It doesn't have to be your brand name that you use on all your signage; you can also use a statement of intent.

ONE PRODUCT: LIMITED EDITION PACKAGING

People love to see what's new. While we might be content with a brand we've used for as long as we can remember, we're often tempted by something different and new because it's interesting. But what if you are so happy with your product you don't want to change anything about it?

The idea

STEAM**CREAM**, a British-Japanese brand, has one product. They make a face, hand and body cream which ticks the right ethical boxes: Vegan, natural, one layer of packaging. It started off in a plain, recyclable (or reusable) aluminium tin, different designs were added to the range, and are now there are over 100.

In the UK, they keep the original plain design in stock, and one intriguingly named Freedom & Discipline, which is decorated with the UK Union Flag, (AKA Union Jack). The others are limited editions and only last until they sell out, all at the same price, apart from the bling-a-ding-dong Swarovski crystal version that sold for ten times more than usual.

Use up the cream and you can keep your paperclips in the packaging. Vogue's beauty blog featured the tins as a cool way to store small things. As repurposing becomes the most creative way to be green, STEAM**CREAM** has become part of the environmental movement. They also keep their customers by sustaining their interest.

This approach will only work if the designs are good. Many of the STEAMCREAM tins are quirkily Japanese–the duck, dog and pig faces (Quack, Bow-Wow and Oink) are particularly unusual for skincare–but most of them are appealing because of their attractiveness. They also run competitions for customers to have their own designs put into production, like Vinyl, a tin that looks like an LP.

An idea like this only works if the product is great quality. Customers might be attracted by good packaging, but they still want good value from what's on the inside.

In practice

- Invite designers to repackage your product.
- Organise competitions to get hold of good designs.
- Provide yourself with reasons to contact the specialist media with a news story each time you bring out a new design.

16 REVIVE A VINTAGE BRAND

Times change, and companies can become outdated. Fashion is fickle. Brands can become dated and disappear from the scene, only to be rediscovered by a new generation who think they are amazingly cool. Reviving a long lost brand can be the start of a new business.

The idea

In France, the Sajou brand was given the kiss of life by an obsessive collector of vintage haberdashery, Frédérique Crestin-Billet. After paying a considerable sum for an old Sajou catalogue, she asked herself what had been so special about the defunct company and started delving into their history. She discovered that the brand name was available, registered it and opened the first Sajou website in 2005 selling Sajou branded embroidery scissors and postcards featuring some of their original designs.

Madame Crestin-Billet used the huge collection of Sajou archive material to create a new company, which retained the spirit of the original brand idea. She also searched for French manufacturers in order to keep her products as authentic as possible, despite the attraction of financial savings to be gained by having them made in China.

The company was immediately successful. It captured a large market in Japan, where the consumers were enamoured with the individuality of the brand. The ornate belle époque designs, which had looked dreadfully out of date from the 1930s to the 1960s, are now appreciated for their intricate details. The products are of high quality and they are expensive, but for serious dressmakers, the price is justifiable.

In practice

- It helps to have a passion for your subject. Other brands that have been brought back to life include perfumers Les Parfums de Rosine and Grossmith, and the fountain pen manufacturer Conway Stewart.
- Visit the British Library online to look for memorable brands that have fallen out of use. Research your family background for business connections.
- Register the trademark once you find the available brand you would like to revive.

17 RAID THE ARCHIVE FOR CLASSICS

Recycling is a great use of resources, and that includes ideas. Not everything works, of course. Some products fell out of favour because they weren't good enough the first time around. Some of our favourite childhood soft drinks will never be seen again because their sweeteners were banned as a health hazard.

If your company does have a history, it's worth searching through the old files and storage boxes for ideas. In a 1950s magazine, I spotted an advertisement from the for the shampoo Pantene Pro-V. At the time, it was marketed as an anti-baldness vitamin shampoo for men. Obviously the ASA would never allow Pantene to claim that it can cure male-pattern baldness these days, so after a lapse of several decades the brand was reinvented as a vitamin shampoo for healthier hair.

The brand name still had value because it was a successful product in many people's memories.

The idea

Perhaps the best known reinvented UK brand is Tango, Britvic's range of canned fizzy drinks. Tango was first brought out in 1950 by Corona, who were bought by the Beecham group in 1958. Beecham's sold their fizzy drinks to Britvic almost three decades later, by which time Tango, the orange flavour in a range of drinks, was pretty much forgotten.

In 1991 in the UK Tango became famous when an advertisement – which most of us remember fondly for its humour – was criticised for promoting violence. As an actor took a sip of his orange Tango drink, an entirely orange almost naked overweight man rushed up to him and slapped him in the face, then ran away. The tagline "You know when you've been Tango'd!" started a cult following. Unfortunately, schoolchildren started to "Tango" each other at the playground, so the advertisement was removed from television and replaced immediately with one featuring the orange man planting a kiss on the drinker's face.

However, the phrase had captured the public's imagination and without the benefit of docial media to connect with customers, Tango built up a relationship with theirs by flashing up phone numbers in their television ads. Fans had to record them on their VCRs, pause at exactly the right moment, and then dial the telephone number to get their free limited-edition cult Tango object.

Apple Tango was given a seductive character and even had its own calendar in the style of the famous Pirelli. But instead of supermodels, it featured cans of fizzy drink.

Blackcurrant Tango was launched in 1996 with an advertisement called St George, an immense production featuring Harrier jump jets, and ending with a challenge to France and the rest of Europe to come up with a better drink.

All these from a dusty old brand name sitting on the back of a shelf.

In practice

- This is a job for people who love nothing more than to burrow into the darkest corners of the basement and dig out material that they find fascinating (but others would be tempted to throw in a skip). Do not allow your de-clutterers is anywhere near this task as they will jettison valuable archives in the quest for tidiness.

- Bring the most interesting finds to your next meeting, and use it to spark new ideas.

- Check the reasons for the brand fell into disuse. If it was only from a lack of support and attention, then the brand could be a potential candidate for revival.

LOGOS 1: LOGOS GO LARGE

Logos are a shorthand for a brand. They encapsulate in one visual symbol everything that the observer knows about that brand. This is one good reason why a brand can't solely rely on its logo to establish its identity. Each customer's opinion of a brand is based on his or her own experience of it: Price, quality, reliability, personality, the behaviour of the people who work for the organisation, all this and more. Logos save us time. When we spot one that we recognise, we can recall the things we know about the brand and make a decision based on past experience. When we spot a logo that is new to us, its design will help us to decide whether or not we want to find out more.

A brand doesn't have to have a logo, but if you want instant recognition, particularly if you are operating internationally where your customers speak different languages and use different alphabets, a logo can come in very handy.

The idea

The McDonald brothers, Richard and Maurice, opened their first restaurant in 1940. In 1953, Richard altered their architect's design for their first fast-food restaurant in Phoenix, Arizona and added two yellow arches, one at each end of the building. (This was against the architect's wishes.) From the correct angle they formed the capital letter M. These became known as the Golden Arches. McDonald also used a double yellow arch in the form of a capital M with their name on all their signage and marketing materials.

The architectural arches are rarely used on McDonald's buildings these days, but tho logo remains. McDonald's corporate logo is now a yellow capital M without the McDonalds' name.

Whether or not you choose to eat their food, you can be certain that wherever you see the Golden Arches it will taste exactly the same and be of a consistent standard, and that the restaurant will be clean. There are times when a confused tourist sees the Golden Arches appear on the horizon and feels delighted to see a familiar symbol in a strange land.

It has taken 70 years for McDonald's logo to achieve its international status as one of the world's most familiar symbols and theirs is an example of how keeping your branding constant, with small changes over the decades to bring it up to date, just keeps building and building.

In practice

- The Golden Arches work because of their distinctive shape and colour. It's bright and it's simple. How will yours look when it's two metres tall?

- You will need planning permission for a logo large enough to be spotted from a distance. If your business is located along a quaint, historic high street you won't get it. McDonald's has adapted their logo to fit local regulations, but in a way that is still recognisable, notably in Hampstead, London, where the entire shopfront had to be redesigned to fit the surroundings, and in Sedona, Arizona, where the arches are turquoise.

- Internationally, your symbol should mean what you intend it to mean. Check with localisation experts, and with people in their own markets, that it doesn't signify something different.

HAVE THE NICEST PEOPLE

A recruitment manager told me once, "Our graduate applicants think that what employers want is someone who's ambitious, full of initiative and willing to take on a lot of responsibility. What we really want are people who will fit in with the team, make the tea when it's their turn and get on with what we ask them to do."

Some companies have realised how important it's to employ pleasant people. Others persist in believing that they need the hardest, meanest most ambitious staff members to be successful. The Harvard Business Review wrote about how one person can destroy a company's positive culture. They called this person "the corporate ass-hole" and recommended that no matter how hardworking or financially successful this person is, they should be removed from the business, or sent for behavioural training to help them fit in. Their research showed that although the bullies had short-term success, long-term they would upset so many clients and colleagues that it would damage the business.

Lush's founder, Mark Constantine, recruits people only if he likes the idea of spending a two hour train journey with them. He regularly travels from Poole, Dorset, to London and back. He would picture himself travelling with a potential candidate along this route. If he can't bear the thought of it, he would recruit someone else no matter how good this person looks on paper.

The idea
One company that takes the pleasantness of its staff seriously is

Singapore Airlines. They were quick to realise that when people are 30,000 feet up in the sky, stuck in a metal tube for up to 18 hours at a stretch, friendly smiling faces can make the experience a pleasure rather than of a pain.

An ad man names Ian Batey came up with the Singapore Girl idea in 1972, and the airline's publicity has emphasised the helpfulness, grace and beauty of their air crew ever since. The Singapore Girls have been wearing a version of the Malayan sarong designed by Pierre Balmain, the Paris fashion designer, since 1968.

Attitudes to women have changed, and the Singapore Girl has been criticised as old-fashioned and demeaning. Singapore Airlines' response has been to employ equally helpful, pleasant men as aircrew, building on on their reputation for superb service from nice people.

In practice

- We've all been on journeys where the staff have made a difference to the atmosphere, whether it's half an hour on a train with a pleasant conductor, or a driver who smiles when we board the bus. We know we'll never return to restaurants with snooty waiters no matter how good the food was. And yet when it comes to recruitment we tend to follow the age old rules of checking to see who's the best qualified or has the most experience. Try changing your recruitment policy, putting yourself in your customer shoes and asking yourself if you would enjoy doing business with that person.

- Lead by example. If staff see that it's fine for managers to shout, bully, and hard sell their way through the day, then they'll behave that way towards their customers. Be pleasant, fair and firm when necessary, and behave towards staff and customers the way you would hope to be treated.

PLAY A TUNE

It takes five musical notes in a row to make a distinctive tune. Played on a particular instrument, or a combination of them, or in a musical style, or sung by a recognisable voice, you've got your own short piece of branding in sound.

The idea

Intel makes computer chips. Their name comes from the the the company name *Int*egrated *El*ectronics Corporation. Not only it's a name that can be easily related to the company's full name, it also happens to be an abbreviation of intelligence. With its Pentium processor in the 1990s, its advertising included a quick, four note tune with a visual showing the words "Intel Inside", often added at the end of a PC manufacturer's television commercial as an extra selling point.

Intel operates in a huge, competitive market, and their aggressively competitive methods have been brought into question. They faced several expensive legal challenges from their competitors in the 2000s.

However, those of us who don't operate in the technology industry would be hard pushed to name one of their competitors; but if someone were to sing you the Intel tune, you'd probably be able to identify them and what they do.

In practice

- If you use radio, TV or sound on your Internet presence, consider adding a tune that encapuslates the mood of your brand.
- Have it composed by a professional jingle writer, who will know how to make it sufficiently distinctive to avoid any copyright infringement.
- Test it to check that it's catchy without being irritating.

21 IT'S WHAT'S INSIDE THAT COUNTS

When a company makes the secret ingredient which creates the difference between an average product and a good one, then they can work with the owner of the finished product to market both brands together.

Look at many foods and cosmetics and you'll find list of what the products don't contain, marketed as a selling point. Instead of distracting people by saying what you don't have, consider the things that you do have which might help your brand stand out.

The idea

Like Pentium, there are a small number of companies who have built a well known brand by working in partnership with the end-product brand owner.

Spandex or elastane is an extremely stretchy, shiny yarn. Lycra is DuPont's elastane brand name. Adding a percentage of elastane to another yarn, such as cotton, to make a jersey fabric, helps the final garment to hold its shape and provides extra support for the wearer.

In the UK, DuPont have made Lycra the generic name, by working with sports clothes and underwear manufacturers, and others who make stretchy things. They'll add an extra label to tell you that you're buying something that contains Lycra, and the percentage there is in the garment. So now we've been educated know what difference 2% or 5% or 10% makes to stretchiness and shine.

What is essentially a trade ingredient has upped its profile and become a brand in its own right.

In practice

- Look for synergy between your brand and your customers, and your suppliers too.
- Is yours the secret ingredient? Work with your customers to unveil it. If you are using secret ingredients, ask your supplier to work together on a joint branding.
- For ingredients that are currently used anonymously, create a brand identity for them. DuPont could happily have supplied clothing manufacturers with unbranded elastane for the last few decades and no-one would know to look out for it.

PRICING 1: SETTING YOUR SELLING PRICE

A big part of how people see your brand is what price you set for what you sell. Their views are influenced by where your brand is positioned against your competitors price wise, whether you have year-round sales, do the occasional three-for-two offers, give discounts, or set a top price and never negotiate.

The idea

You can base your pricing on a combination of these four things:

Costs

Customers

Competition

Corporate strategy

Most importantly, you've got to cover your costs or you'll go out of business.

There's a pricing system called cost plus, which has been in operation since Victorian times, and which some companies today still use to set their prices. It's a good basis to make sure that your costs are covered, but it's not enough. These days companies generally look at what their customers are prepared to pay and what their competitors charge, and then influence prices according to what they're intending to do with their company in future.

The cost plus pricing method basically involves adding up all the costs to get an annual total, then adding a percentage profit on top to work out the selling price. For example, many department stores first total up the fixed costs – such as rental, electricity, water, staff costs, maintenance fees – before adding 200% to the cost of each product they sell to get a selling price.

Using cost plus makes sure that you include all your costs, and add a mark-up to put you into profit. After that, you have a certain amount of flexibility.

While customers are generally happy to get a bargain, it's not true that if you lower the price they will buy more. There is a famous urban myth that at one London department store, if a product didn't sell, their strategy was to double the price. If something costs more, up to a certain point customers will assume that it is better quality. So if quality is what they're looking for, they will search out a higher price not a lower one.

People do feel loyal to brands that they trust, but will often be tempted away by something new, interesting and cheaper. If the new brand disappoints them, they'll be back, so there's no reason to be panicked into cutting your own prices, although you may decide on a tactical temporary discount.

An organisation planning to sell out and shut down will act very differently from one which intends to invest in new property, expand overseas or buy out its competitors. All these things influence your pricing.

And your prices influence your brand identity.

In practice

- Calculate your costs, and unless you are running a temporary tactical campaign, make sure that your prices are going to cover all your expenses and give you sufficient profit to continue trading into the next year.

- Evaluate your brand position in terms of price, quality, value and other influences. Set a price that is consistent with your position in the market.
- Do you want to change the way your customers see your brand? You can change your prices to make a brand statement, but be prepared to change them back.

PRICING 2: NEVER DISCOUNT

Companies can choose to take a flexible position on pricing or a firm one. Some companies never reduce the price of their goods or services. There are different reasons for this, and it can have different results.

The idea

Set a fair price for your products and services. Explain to your customers you do not give discounts because you believe that you're giving them good value.

The luxury luggage manufacturer (turned catwalk fashion brand) Louis Vuitton never give discounts for their handbags. They keep a standard range of classic styles, then create limited editions, which, once sold out, will not be manufactured again. They also run a well funded advertising and PR campaign to make sure that their products are sought after, and are seen on the arms of many an A-list celebrity.

At the more affordable end of the market M.A.C cosmetics do the same. So do Lush.

The bakery at the end of my street runs on the same basis, hand making daily batches which generally sell out by mid-afternoon. On Saturdays, there is a queue and halfway down the street from Parker's the Bakers (Established 1912) because customers have learnt that they've to be there early to get what they want.

In practice

- Balance economies of scale from manufacturing more than you need, with reducing the risk of overproduction by making slightly fewer products available than you forecast your customers would buy. The more experience you have, as in the case of long established organisations like Parkers and Louis Vuitton, the more accurate your forecasts are going to be.

- When you build your brand identity on never discounting, never ever discount.

- Only take this stance if you can be certain you'll be able to stick with it.

24 PRICING 3: BE THE CHEAPEST

It's generally recognised in the world of business that adopting the brand position of the cheapest in your market can never be a long-term strategy.

There is always someone who can find a way to come into your market and undercut you; even if they don't stay in the business long, they could be there long enough to damage your reputation and force you to reduce your prices.

The idea

John Lewis has been using the slogan "Never Knowingly Undersold" since 1925. It completely baffled me when I was a child. It means: "As far as we are aware, no one gives better value than we do." In these days of Internet price comparison, John Lewis had to reconsider what to do with this line. Competitors deliberately targeted the items they sold, and reduced their own prices forcing John Lewis to do the same in order to keep their decades old promise.

John Lewis would have had to restrict their stock to obscure brands that none of their competitors sold, their own brand and undiscounted products like upmarket cosmetics, or to change their decades-old strategy. They chose to tweak their principle of pricing their products. Their slogan now refers to the total value and quality they give, not just the price.

If you want to build a reputation for having the lowest prices in the market, then something's got to give. It's either quality, margins or range or all three. Or you bump up your prices by selling insurance at the checkout. Although very few customers will state out loud that finding the cheapest price is not important to them, the reality is that they will shop where they feel comfortable, and price is only one factor in anyone's buying decision.

In practice

- Bear in mind that although people will say that price strongly influences what they decide to buy, they won't buy something they don't like no matter how cheap it is.

- You can earn a reputation for being the cheapest, just by telling people that you are. Some supermarkets choose to discount a small range of products and kick up a huge fuss about this, giving the impression of offering good value. One option is to have a discounted range, but not the entire stock.

- There will always be someone who will come in and undercut you, and undermine your brand positioning. Unless you are certain you'll be able to hold your position, being the cheapest in the market is a really bad idea. (But it's in this book because despite the risks it's still popular.)

PRICING 4: KEEP A BARGAIN BASEMENT

Between never discounting and offering the lowest prices in the market, there's a good balance for brands which want to build a reputation for offering good value, without the risk of slicing margins too thinly.

Retailers, both real shops and online, can attract customers who are searching for a bargain but keep their discounted area separate from their new, full price stock.

The idea

These days there are whole shops, and even entire shopping malls, devoted to bargain basement style retailing. TK Maxx (and in the US TJ Maxx) take stock from previous seasons and the overstocks from the current season, pack them closely together on basic displays and serve as the discount department for some very well-known manufacturers, and the less famous ones too. Manufacturers who don't have their own stores can use these outlets to shift their end of season stock, without damaging their own brand positioning. Because everyone who goes there knows that this is a compromise. You get good quality, but not at the same time as the fashionistas.

Out of town retail parks have popped up, from the basic to the super deluxe. This is where you will find high street stores, from Cadbury and the Body Shop to Smythson and Paul Smith, with branches which only sell sale goods and seconds.

Web shops are ideal places to keep virtual bargain basements. Customers click on one button to take them into separate department, which web designers can brand differently with a bargain look and feel, inviting bargain hunters in to clear out the back of the warehouses.

In practice

- People love bargains, and if your brand has a reputation for being high quality, it'll make your customers very happy to get their hands on one of your products at a discount. It won't damage your brand and it will help to build brand loyalty.

- Online, it's simple to create a bargain basement as part of your website. You can bring it to the front page during the sale seasons of January and July, and relegate it to a less prominent place for the rest of the year.

- In terms of your overall branding, keep your emphasis on your current lines and full price stock. Unless you run a 100% discount store, your bargain basement shouldn't take over your pricing strategy.

26 PRICING 5: GIVE GREAT VALUE

Value, like beauty, is in the eye of the beholder. Often, good value and low price are used to mean the same thing, but they actually aren't. Value is a combination of price, quality, usefulness and how many times you can use what you've bought; it can also include the extras that come with it.

If one person buys a pair of bright pink trainers at £50 and wears them every day for months until they fall apart, then she's got good value. If another person buys the same pair during a sale at £15, and then decides she has made a terrible mistake and she's never going to wear them, leaves them in the cupboard and finally gives them away, she didn't get good value at all.

So giving good value, and building a brand identity around that, includes making sure that you are selling your wares to people who really appreciate them.

The idea

The Magic Marker is a pen favoured by graphic designers and layout artists worldwide. They are now made in Japan, they've adopted the generic name "magic" for a marker pen, just as the Russians called a pencil a *karandash* (from the Swiss manufacturer Caran D'Ache). You can buy them in around 150 shades, and in sets of 12 for particular uses, like portraits, landscapes or architects' drawings. Individually, they cost around four to five times more than standard marker pens.

There are alternatives, mostly from Japanese companies, but the Magic Marker keeps its place as the one that gives the best value. So yes, designers and artists still choose them. But if you're going to be using them to write on flipchart paper, why would you pay four times more for a pen that does the same thing as a standard flipchart marker? Because of the value they give.

The meeting rooms of the world are littered with empty husks of flipchart markers. If – like me – you often run workshops and turn up to find that even the nice new pens don't last the day – you'll appreciate pens which are still flowing after ten days' hard work. And the participants appreciate it too. A good workshop can be ruined by the squeak of dried up pens; thoughts dry up at the same time. (Although I did see jaws drop once when I mentioned that my pack of 12 pens had cost me £50.)

So for me, this is a great example of great value. People appreciate it when they get to work with good quality materials, so although they are an investment, they easily justify the cost in the long run.

So if you do have a brand that you know is of great value, how do you make that known?

In practice

- Point out where the value lies in choosing your brand over the competition. That way your customers can justify the initial expense as they make their decision.
- Without comparing yourself directly to other brands – as this usually puts your brand in a bad light as well – let customers know that your brand has added benefits, including that it pays for itself several times over.

27 PRICING 6: BE THE MOST EXPENSIVE

It's about prestige. You can't just put your prices up without matching them with quality, and expect customers to pay. But by being expensive you are making a branding statement. It positions you right at the top of the luxury market. Not everyone wants to be there, but when you occupy that slot it's something you can draw attention to.

The idea

Breaking records attract publicity, including to prices. Each time a house breaks the top price barrier, it's reported in the press. If you are at the top end of the market, you can use your price positioning to get people talking about you. Bear in mind that you'll be criticised for encouraging extravagance ("fat cat") once you attract media attention for being expensive, but if that's where you want your brand to be, then go ahead.

As customers, we tend to believe that if something is exceptionally expensive, it must be exceptionally good. This is a very cynical view of pricing policy, but there is a ring of truth about it.

For high prices to be sustainable, you really do have to keep your quality top notch. You can only fool somebody once, and that really isn't a good business strategy, but if your brand does offer exceptional quality, then there's no need to be afraid of setting a high price for it. For decades, Joy perfume by Jean Patou was known as the world's most expensive. Now the slot's been taken by Clive Christian's Imperial Majesty, but the price ($215,000) is mostly for the diamond studded bottle.

In practice

- If you have an expensive brand and you can justify the price in quality terms, tell the press all about it and get yourself talked about.
- Make sure that all your staff, especially your sales people, feel comfortable with the pricing and are proud of what you're offering.
- Be courageous. Explain why it's expensive and give your potential customers the reasons they should buy it.

28 CUSTOMER TIERS

Picture a theatre. Everyone is there to see the same show, but facing the stage you have the stalls, the circle, the upper circle and balcony, nicknamed "the gods" because you're so high up, you're closer to heaven than earth. Some tickets might cost 10 times more than the others but everyone has bought almost the same experience. The front stalls and the circle cost more because the view and sound are better.

Brands can include more people in their market by offering their customers different tiers, different price levels for a similar experience.

The idea

Fashion brands are past masters of arranging their customers in tiers. From the 1930s Paris couture houses also sold perfumes, and this proved extremely profitable by broadening their market to a much wider group of women than those who could afford the dresses.

In the 1960s Pierre Cardin broke the rules by launching a prêt-à-porter (ready to wear) range and was thrown out of the couturiers' association for his bad behaviour. Although he was soon invited back, once his former colleagues observed his financial success. He'd made his designs available to a much wider audience. Those who could afford couture still felt that they were the ones with the real Pierre Cardin clothes, so he still retained that tier of customers.

In practice

- This is a lot easier from the top down. You can create tiers below a well-known, luxury brand, but building upwards is harder. Honda motorcycles built upwards, from their little scooters to their superbikes, but they faced a lot of scepticism and had to prove themselves over the decades through sheer quality and reliability.

- You can create tiers by extending your brand into more affordable but consistent markets. The Christian Dior couture line still does catwalk shows, but the company makes its profits from accessories, perfume and make up.

- Know where to draw the line. Cardin's brand extension into thousands of different licensed products weakened his fashion brand identity.

29 ⏺ BE GOOD

It's called transparency, allowing everyone to know what's happening inside your organisation, as well as letting them see the face you present to the outside world. It means being open and honest in all your actions, so if you were scrutinised more closely investigated, the way you really operate will match up to what you say about yourself. With the Internet, it's possible for everyone with a connection to know about your wrongdoings in a very short space of time.

Consider the infamous "wheelie bin cat lady" from 2010, caught on CCTV dumping a cat inside a wheelie bin for no particular reason, as she admitted later. The film flashed round the globe in no time. The same thing happens to organisations.

The idea

When independent designers have their work copied by large retailers, their stories are very quickly transmitted through social media networks because we hate to see big guys picking on small guys. It's known as "copywrong". In the UK and artist known as Hidden Eloise had her work copied, and the final result appeared in the stationery chain Paperchase. Although Paperchase believed they were buying original work, and denying any wrongdoing at first, the Internet campaign meant that they had to reinvestigate, then later apologise.

Decades ago, it was standard practice for companies not to admit that they were at fault, even when they were caught. Now when something goes wrong, organisations recognise that the best thing to do is stand up and admit their mistake, then quickly put it right and tell everyone.

Everyone makes mistakes, that's just human, and companies are run by human beings after all. Customers will accept an apology as long as it's genuine, and quick. No-one likes to be kept in the dark, or to feel that their being made fools of, as in the Ratner case.

Talking of Ratner's, brands can be damaged so badly they never recover if their owners allow their reputations to be dragged through the dirt. If you fall in, climb out, get washed and get on with it.

In practice

- If in doubt, behave as though the BBC were filming you for a documentary. With the speed at which information travels these days, if you behave badly, you will be found out in no time.
- When you make a mistake, admit it quickly, put things right and apologise.
- Think of your customers as your friends and family. If you wouldn't recommend your products and services to people you are close to, then improve them until you would.

MOVE THE GOALPOSTS

There are times when a brand will make such a radical change to its product that it forces all the others who are playing on the same pitch to pull their socks up and try a lot harder, or give up and go home. What customers thought was normal or accepted as the best they were going to get, suddenly looks outdated and meagre compared with the new stuff.

The idea

In the 1970s, you were lucky if an ice cream shop offered more than three flavours: vanilla, chocolate and strawberry. You could add a Cadbury's Flake (a "99") or monkey blood, a red topping with an unidentifiable fruit flavour. Maybe you would stumble across the occasional chocolate chip or rum 'n' raisin. A very smart establishment might sell lemon and orange sorbets (sherbets in the US).

Then came Baskin-Robbins. They were established in the US in 1945, so for Americans 31 flavours probably seemed normal, but to us in the UK it was if a spaceship had landed from another planet bringing previously unimagined variety.

Naturally, they encountered the neo-sceptics who wondered why anyone needed so many different flavours, and what was wrong with vanilla anyway? Baskin-Robbins had moved the goalposts so far, they'd rewritten the rules of the game.

In practice

- It's an opportunity to get talked about, to hammer home your brand values. It's also risky. Others have probably tried and failed. If you can, test the idea first.
- You're building on new ground, so make sure that the foundations are firm, that you're ready, that your quality is up to scratch and that you'll delight everyone who comes along to find out what you're up to.
- You need to grab the attention of the opinion formers, back it up with a PR campaign.

31 BE AN EXEMPLARY EMPLOYER

It's a fact of life that bad news travels faster than good. Organisations treating their employees badly can be local gossip, or go global on the Internet. In the 21st Century, everyone involved with a brand, from the customers and suppliers to the employees, shareholders and pension fund trustees, expects to be treated well, and will speak out if they are disappointed.

Branding is not just about the ideal image presented to customers, it has to be more than skin deep. There's a television programme, Undercover Boss, in which the managing director or the owner goes to work at his or own company as a junior employee to find out what it's really like. What would you find out if you tried it?

The idea

What staff say about their own brands carries a lot of weight. Would your staff recommend your products? Do they encourage people they know and like to apply for jobs?

In the UK, there's an annual survey in the Sunday Times, the Top 100 Companies To Work For, run by the organisation, Best Companies. Companies have to register to take part – no-one gets a surprise when they find out they've been nominated – and employees fill in a detailed survey giving facts and opinions about their workplace. The organisers will visit these organisations to check the credibility of the survey findings, and to ensure that no overbearing bosses are standing over their employees to force them to tick the correct boxes.

To come high up on the Sunday Times List is a benefit to companies. If you have a great reputation for being a good employer that runs a happy, successful organisation, naturally you'll attract more people. And being a great company to work for helps to keep staff loyal, which saves on recruitment and training.

If your people are miserable at work, they tell their friends and family about it. It's bad for your brand as well as morale.

In practice

- Change comes from the top down. Set a great example for your people to follow.
- For a brand, the aim is to be talked about in a positive way, to have staff saying what a great time they have at work.
- There are many companies who specialise in organisational culture, working with management to change it for the better. Use one.

BEING GREEN 1: REUSABLE PACKAGING

There are two reasons to put your products into useful, reusable packaging. One is that it doesn't go into landfill because people will keep it, and the other is that things with your brand name on will hang around for longer.

The idea

The Japanese package things beautifully, but can get carried away with layer upon layer of delightful but expensive presentation. For example, you might be offered bean paste sweets with a wrapping of cellophane covering beautiful paper wrapped around a box that contains individually double wrapped confectionery.

This is a relatively modern move. Traditionally, the Japanese would present their gifts in a woven cloth; you would unwrap them, then give the cloth, called a furushiki, back to the giver.

The cosmetics company Lush has built its reputation of making solid products which need the very minimum of packaging, so they can spend their budget on lovely natural materials instead of containers. Most cosmetics costs are 80% packaging/20% materials. At Lush it's 0–20% packaging/80–100% materials.

As Lush became successful in Japan, their Japanese staff felt uncomfortable selling unpackaged products as it's rude not to wrap products, and even worse to present naked gifts. This was obviously an issue that needed to be solved, as Japan was overtaking the UK as Lush's biggest market. The Japanese gifts team presented the idea of gift-wrapping with furushikis as a solution to the problem.

Now at Lush you can have your gifts wrapped in a specially designed range of furushikis. You can reuse it or you can wear it as a scarf if you prefer. The UK name – "The Knot-Wrap" and it's strapline, "We're Knot-wrapping your presents" – were devised by Ruth Andrade, from Brazil and Pia Long, from Finland – to make it a truly international campaign, that helps to support the Lush brand's green credentials.

In practice

- This is not just thinking outside the box, it's thinking with no box at all. It took a few attempts to get the Knot-Wrap idea to work, so get some creative thinkers together and give them time.
- Bear in mind what the customers say they need, but don't let that hold you back. Consider their needs then have to courage to do something better.
- It's one thing to make reusable packaging, and another to get people to reuse it. Reward customers with an incentive to bring their packaging back for a refill. (By the way, this doesn't work for liquids. Not allowed. Washed out bottles don't pass safety standards.)

BEING GREEN 2: ECO BAGS

When I was a kid, you had to pay for a carrier bag, unless you went to a really posh shop. Supermarkets never handed out free ones. You took your own shopping bags with you. That's all changed. Shop owners started to see the advantage of the free advertising they got by sending people out of their shops carrying their names and logos.

In the developed world, where there are ways and means of recycling bags, the environmental impact is bad, but in the developing world it's appalling. Cheap plastic carrier bags are trapped in hedges and trees, blow about on beaches and are eaten by birds, mammals and fish where they cause their early deaths.

Now, there are two forces working together to reduce the numbers of free bags being given out: companies are looking to cut costs, and more people want to protect our environment by reducing waste and landfill.

We're now using shopping bags again, but this time they've been rebranded: it's the era of the eco-bag. There are ecological advantages to using eco-bags because they reduce the numbers of plastic carrier bags, and there are branding advantages too.

The idea

In France the hypermarket Carrefour have fabulous eco-bags, brightly coloured with strong graphics and slogans, tough, long lasting and recognisable. Customers buy them to make a statement as well as carry their shopping, and heir durability and good design make sure that they're used regularly.

The most sought after eco-bag in the UK was Sainsbury's 2007 Anya Hindmarsh bag, a limited edition canvas bag printed with the slogan "I'm not a plastic bag." It was produced with social enterprise We Are What We Do. Unfortunately, it was a limited edition. As it was featured in style magazines, it became a sought after item which was then sold on eBay for up to 40 times its original cost. With the news coverage this generated, people looked a little more closely into the story and found that the bag had been manufactured in China and shipped to the UK. Eco-warriors declared that it ought to have been made locally to minimise its carbon footprint. Others argued that one green step is better than none. It certainly attracted a lot of attention, and the bag became the "must have" fashion item of the month.

Some aren't that useful; the cheapest are cotton, flat, with room for a couple of books and nothing more. They make a statement, but can't be used regularly enough to claim eco status; they're just one more thing on its way to landfill.

In practice

- Offer to sell your customers an eco-bag instead of giving away free ones. If your'e serious about your ethics, do it right. Have yours made in organic cotton, by a fair trade cooperative.
- Make it practical and durable. For example, handles should be long enough to go over the shoulder, but not so long that it trails on the ground when you carry it by hand.

- Make it attractive. Good design often costs about the same as bad design, so make it good-looking enough for your customers to want to use yours, not someone else's eco-bag. That way your eco-bags will last, be used often, and they say good things about you and your brand.

FEARLESS DESIGNS

Get yourself stared at. A brand has to be daring to smash through the accepted norms and do something completely different. But it certainly gets you noticed. As ever there's a risk that if you're too bold, you'll reduce the number of people who want to buy your goods. Then again, you can always go for the customer tier approach, get known for a totally outrageous approach, then add the slightly outrageous to broaden your appeal without reducing your brand's impact.

The idea

United Nude is an ethical shoe manufacturer whose fabulous footwear is collaboration between two men named Rem and Galahad. Rem Koolhass is a Dutch architect who designed United Nude's Möbius shoe in an attempt to win back his lost girlfriend, so the story goes. Galahad Clark is the seventh generation shoemaker from the UK company, Clark's, who took over the Terra Plana ethical shoe brand in 2002.

The Möbius series is moderately outrageous, but United Nude went further still with their Abstract and Eamz ranges. Have a look at www.unitednude.com to get the picture.

These shoes are not cheap. I've seen more affordable copies and they fall apart. Structurally, these shoes need Rem Koolhaas's architectural input to keep their integrity. But they are successful, because they're worn by people who see them as an extension of their own personality; they like to feel a little outrageous themselves.

They're so unusual, they make news. Even if it's just fashion news, it all helps to build a stronger brand identity.

In practice

- Being talked about in the press for the right reasons is great. If you've got something that people will stare at, then get the PR people on to it.

- According to the United Nude story, it was Rem having his heart broken that inspired him to make the Möbius shoe. Even at your worst times, you can have some amazing ideas while your mind is exploring places it doesn't usually visit. Don't dump them when you're feeling better, use them.

TELL YOUR PEOPLE WHAT YOU STAND FOR

Make sure that everyone who works for you knows your brand well. They should know the direction of the organisation and the core values behind your brand. Your staff is in the best position to spread good things about your brand, and how they talk about your products will have some impact on your brand position in the market.

The idea

There's a story about a man who was working at NASA. It might be true. The tale is that President Kennedy visited the building and asked a cleaner what he did for a living and he said, "I help to put a man on the moon."

When you're willing to stand up and be counted, and when you know that all your colleagues feel the same, then you've got a successful brand on your hands, being built from the inside out.

So, if you asked your colleagues, "Do you know what our organisation does? What does our brand mean to you? Are you proud of it?" If they feel connected to the centre and would be happy to recommend to their friends and family the things your organisation provides, and stand up for what it represents, it's working. If not, and it's just a job and just about bringing home the cash, then it's time to spread the message. Have a look at the Sunday Times Top 100 Companies; these are places where the employees think it's great to work. Visit their websites. What do they do differently?

In practice

- If you've got people who think they only do data entry, or only answer the phones then they aren't part of the brand. Contacting them personally is an investment, but it's good value.
- Put your organisation's stories on the intranet, in buildings, on noticeboards, and write to people individually, on paper, at home.
- We often forget that other people don't know everything we know about our organisation. It doesn't do any harm to repeat your brand stories and remind people of what you stand for.

LIVE YOUR BRAND VALUES

You've got a book about branding in your hands, so you're either working on one, studying, or planning to set up a new organisation. If you already own a brand or you work for one, then you're not just part of it, you represent it to the outside world.

There's a well known beauty brand that praises natural beauty; the idea was developed by someone who prefers Botox herself. A case of do what I say, not what I do. Its customers might feel let down if they knew.

The idea

Ecotricity is a sustainable power company in the UK. It invests profits into sustainable energy sources like wind turbines and have their own eco forest near their Gloucestershire turbine at Lynch Knoll. They have partnerships with other green organisations to strengthen their brand, and carry out constructive projects. So you might be surprised to hear that their MD and founder Dale Vince, drives a 170 mph sports car to work.

However, the Nemesis is an electric car, powered by sustainable electricity. (Technically, you can only be sure that your energy is sustainable if you disconnect from the National Grid, "going off-grid", but Ecotricity supply the wind-power to the grid, then use some for the car.) Dale uses it to show that there is an exciting future in sustainable energy, and to turn heads. It is an astoundingly beautiful and expensive vehicle, and it makes his point. Green cars don't have to be ugly, slow and dull.

In practice

- Look at what your brand stands for and see how you can apply it to yourself. If they don't fit the way you like to live, find – or create – a brand that does.
- If someone says to you, "You don't seem like the kind of person who would..." ask why. Our own view of our identity is often completely different other people's, as Robert Burns wrote in his poem To A Louse:

  "O would some power the giftie gie us to see ourselves
  as others see us."

- Bear in mind that whenever and wherever you are representing your brand, you are part of something bigger.

37 E-BRANDING 1: BUILDING YOUR BRAND'S WEBSITE

For your online branding to work, stick to the same principles as all your other work. Remind yourself of your values and your identity. Back in the 90s, when less than 1% of the UK population had access to the Internet, there were some dreadful websites built, even for well known brands. Back then things were different. Now, there's no excuse.

Your website should add extra layers of what your brand stands for, and reflect your values. If it contradicts them, then change it. If your brand depends on its reputation for great customer service, then make sure that you reply to emails straight away, and make it easy to contact you.

The idea

The fantastic thing about websites is that you can change them every minute if you need to, and if you can afford it; you can also make masses of information available at very little extra cost. That's the biggest advantage over a printed paper brochure or catalogue, but it doesn't necessarily replace them. Browsing through pages you can see things you weren't looking for, but might like; with most websites you have to know what you're looking for then search for it.

At its most basic, a website is like the online version of your business card; it shows that you really are who you say you are. We all know that online we can choose the identity we want, but with your brand, stick to the real one, and use all the advantages that the web has to offer to reach new people and give them the information they need.

In practice

- Reflect your brand's values in what you offer online.
- Use your corporate colours, but don't plaster them on too thickly. You want to make your site easily accessible, and pleasant to visit. Use your logo, and have your site designed in the same style as your other marketing materials.
- Write the way you would speak to your customers; that way your website seems like the continuation of a conversation.

38 E-BRANDING 2: CUSTOMER EMAILS

As a general rule, unless their work is related to the communications industry, people born after 1983 don't use email that often for their personal messages. They use social media and online messaging. But people born before then use email regularly.

The idea

If your customers are aged around 30 to 55, then you stand a good chance of reaching them with an email, as long as you're using software with the right tools to get your messages through personal and company firewalls.

Get it right, and you'll see an instant flow of visitors to your website as soon as your email reaches people's inboxes. Get it wrong and they'll either ignore you or unsubscribe.

It's greener to send emails. You can save on postage and paper (and vans) by using an email address instead of a postal address. You can use your email software's analytical tools to tell you how many people opened it, deleted it, or deleted it without opening it, and how many chose to unsubscribe.

Most of us get with a daily email flood of things that we have subscribed to, let alone all the other junk that appears in there from people who don't follow the law, and those who our deliberately breaking it to see if they can raid our bank accounts and steal our identity. At busy times, we scroll through the inbox and only read the ones that look important.

I recommend that you make your emails and social media:

- interesting
- useful
- entertaining
- valuable
- amusing
- and preferably a combination of at least two of those things.

Your customers' time is valuable; if you waste it, you'll annoy them and they'll start to associate your brand with feeling irritated.

Give them something that adds to their day, which they might value enough to forward to a friend, and you'll go up in their estimation. Measure your responses carefully. Notice if you send an email that gets forwarded, and do more like that. If you send one that gets you a swarm of unsubscribers, change your method.

In practice

- Give your email a subject line that will get your readers' attention, and make sure they know it's from you. People are more likely to open one from the Jilly at the Tasty Chocolate Company, than the same email that says it's from Jilly.
- Follow the Data Protection Act rules.
- Decide how regularly you want to send emails then stick to it: monthly, weekly or daily, or only six-monthly if that's how often you have something interesting to say.
- Measure your responses carefully. Notice if you send an email that gets forwarded, and do more like that. If you send one that gets you a swarm of unsubscribers, change your method.

THE STAMP

You can bank on everyone born before 1950 opening every letter you send them. People younger than that will assess what the industry knows as DM, direct mail, and decide whether to open it or put it straight into the recycling. Some of us put it all in a pile and save it until the end of the month when it's time to catch up with the paperwork. Part of the problem is that brand owners are too busy trying to save money when sending out thousands of envelopes at one time, so they don't put anything on the outside of the envelope that might tempt the receiver to open it.

How can you interest people enough to make them open yours?

The idea

Send a personal letter with a stamp on it.

In projects I've done, using a stamp – even with a computer printed address label – we've had up to 12 times more responses than the organisations involved would normally expect.

Just this week I got one of those things from someone who claims to have millions of dollars and needs your bank account to put it into, and will share the proceeds when it all works out nicely. This one claimed to have done the legal work for a distant relative of mine, in China. The other several hundred of these have come by email. This one came by post, with a stamp. If the scammers have moved their evil ways to the postal system, that proves it's much more effective than sending emails.

In practice

- Letters with stamps on go to the top of the pile to be opened first.
- To build a personal relationship with a customer, and demonstrate that at some point a human being touched the letter you're sending, sign it by hand and put a stamp on it. You're a lot more likely to get a response.

WHY NOT STICK WITH THE GENERIC?

Generally, an organisation can set a higher price for a branded product and make a higher profit, even if it's pretty much the same quality as a generic one.

The idea

Not all products and services are branded. In my first aid kit ,there are some Boot's Antiseptic Wipes. Boot's is a brand, the name of the UK chemist shop chain and manufacturing company. They have sub brands like Boot's No 7 make-up, and also sell their own generic products, like Boot's own brand soluble aspirins – which are cheaper than branded ones – and the antiseptic wipes.

If they wanted to make their wipes stand out from anyone else's, they could perhaps call them Swipeys, and launch an advertising campaign to repeat the name enough times to make people remember it. So they would invest in the publicity, and then hope to make more profit because customers would come into Boots, look at what's available and say to themselves, "I'd better get the Swipeys because I've heard of them."

The reason to create a brand rather than use the generic word, like the Apple iPhone rather than just the Apple SmartPhone, is to make it stand out from the rest. There are lots of smart phones, but only Apple can make an iPhone because Apple has protected the name using intellectual property (IP) law.

There are plenty of industries where it's normal to stay with the generic, especially if they are fast-changing, and products are short lived, like fashion.

There, the brands are the company names from Primark to Prada, but you don't get any of them trying to add a brand name to a product like a skirt or a belt or a T-shirt.

There, the companies invest in building a brand reputation around their organisation's name. Prada for luxury and style, Primark for cheap and cheerful, bang up to the minute fashions.

In practice

- You have to invest to build a brand identity, to create a recognisable product or service that stands out from the rest. So you might choose to stick with the generic term.

- Once you have a legally registered brand, be prepared to protect it using intellectual property law. This is a serious financial investment.

- The benefits are that your products and services are easier to sell, once you have your brand identity in place, and you might be able to charge more for them in order to recoup your investment, but this isn't guaranteed.

41 HELP THE MEDIA

The most valuable publicity is to be recommended by someone you trust. Second best is to be recommended by the media.

The idea

To get mentions in the press and the other media, it's important to build relationships with journalists. Bloggers too, but we'll about that separately. When there's something new to say about a brand, organisations usually send a press release. But then you have to hope that journalists will pay attention to your press release not the other hundreds arriving on their desks and into their inboxes.

Of course journalists are busy, and often companies think they'll be too busy to pick up the phone. On the other hand journalists like everyone else have a job to do. They have a page to fill with words and pictures they believe will interest their own customers, their readers, so don't be put off. You can help them to do their job by giving them a useful, interesting story.

Whether you use a PR agency or have your own in-house people, when you launch something new make sure it fits in with the press calendar – monthly magazines are working up to six months in advance on their features – and that your events don't clash with more important dates in the diary.

In practice

- Invite journalists to experience what it is you do, so they understand what makes you different. People are much more likely to write about products and services that they've experienced and enjoyed.
- Provide press releases which give all the information that a journalist needs, with a new angle to the story. After you have sent in your press release, follow up with a phone call to check what else you can do to help.
- Tell the truth.

MAKE FRIENDS
WITH THE MEDIA

Over and above providing the press with whatsoever they need, and building a helpful professional relationship, remember that there are going to be influenced on an emotional level by whether or not they like what your brand is up to. Research in neuroscience these days proves that none of us can make a decision without engaging the brain's emotional centres so being studiously businesslike and professional, and ignoring your brand's personality, could work against you.

The idea

When you hit it off with one of your press contacts, be friendly. There are different levels of friendship, you might not invite all your press friends to your house for tea, but you might go around the corner from the office for a coffee and brand owners often take the press out for lunch.

Help your press contacts to experience your brand. Technically all they need to write about you is the information you give and a photograph, but take this further if you can. Film companies organise viewings, wine companies organise tastings, publishers send out early review copies of their books. Most brands are expected to send out the real product in advance, although if it's very expensive they'll want to back again after photography.

At a press launch, one August, for that year's Christmas range I was talking to a beauty journalist who had already been to two other events that day. She told me that the previous year she'd been to a smart Paris perfume house event and they had given her the entire new range to take back to the office for photography, with their press releases. This included her mum's favourite fragrance, which she wrapped up and handed over on Christmas Day.

Later she got a phone call from her mother, who said she couldn't smell the perfume at all. When the journalist called the company, she found out that these were dummy bottles filled with water.

So technically, the perfume company was providing the journalists with what they needed: The information and the packaging for the picture. But they were shooting their own brand identity in the foot by coming over as cheapskates. There were also missing a great opportunity for the journalists to write their own emotional responses to the perfume.

In practice

- When you have the opportunity to be generous, take it.
- Go beyond the merely professional, because it's a brand's emotional attributes that help people decide whether they like it enough to spend money on it.
- Journalists have long memories.

WHEN IT ALL GOES RIGHT, STAY WITH IT

All organisations hope that they can capture people's attention in a good way with their brand identity. To remember the brand name, the catchphrase, for sales to double in a year, and to generate a second profitable business from the merchandise is almost unheard of. But that's what happened to Compare The Market.

The idea

Compare the Market's meerkats advertising is a great example. Meerkats with Russian accents, getting annoyed at people for accidentally visiting their website comparethemeerkat.com when they are really looking for cheap car insurance. The catchphrase, "simples", pronounced with frustration and in a Russian accent, has made it straight into the English language. It is officially allowed in Scrabble – despite an argument in one of the ads when Sergei didn't want Aleksandr to use it – as it's the plural of simple, a noun meaning a herbal remedy.

The agency VCCP created Aleksandr the Russian meerkat, which was then turned into a brilliantly lifelike CGI model by Passion Pictures. You can buy the Aleksandr soft toy and his "autobiography" A Simples Life.

The original ads have been followed up with War and Peace style epics about how meerkats from Africa ended up in Russia. There are ads filmed in the fictional village of Meerkova. The spoof website comparethemeerkat.com gets millions of visitors But the important point is that their real site, comparethemarket.com doubled its business in the year the ads came out.

In a recent campaign, television ads promise soft toys – 100% cute – to everyone who buys their insurance through Compare the Market. The Russian meerkats arrive at the homes of Compare the Market customers to present them with their gifts. These ads also entertaining, you actually look forward to the breaks in the television programmes hoping you get to see another.

The original creative idea was sheer genius. Combining something rather dull – comparing insurance prices – with something people love to watch on television, meerkats.

In practice

- The best creative ideas come from combining two other ideas in an unusual way.
- When you're successful with one idea, build on it rather than putting all your resources into having another successful idea.
- Creative people get bored with their old ideas a lot more quickly than customers do; that's why they deserve their place in the creative team. Use your idea until it shows signs of becoming less successful. When you've found the winning formula, keep stirring the mixture.

44 CARRIER BAGS, IN COLOUR

With the rise of consumerism, shopping as a leisure activity and buying things for pleasure rather than necessity, the carrier bag has become the norm. While it's greener for shoppers to take their own canvas bags out with them when they're off to buy something, carrier bags are probably here to stay.

As far as brands are concerned, they remind people that you're there by serving as portable billboards. For brand awareness, carrier bags are brilliant.

The idea

In New York, the most famous carriers are Bloomingdale's Little Brown Bag, Medium Brown Bag and Big Brown Bag. They're so well known they don't even say Bloomingdale's on them. They give the paper ones away with purchases, and you can buy the fabric shoppers.

In London, Harrods used to dominate the branded shopping bag market with their olive green and gold branded shoppers. Now, it's Selfridges bright yellow that stands out on Oxford Street and beyond. You can spot a Selfridges bag from the other end of a train platform. Liberty's purple is distinctive too, Nike's is red with a swoosh.

People will always come out without their eco-bags, and retailers have to find a way to help them get their shopping home. Whatever style you choose, make sure your brand can be spotted easily.

In practice

- Use your name.
- Use your corporate colours.
- Use your logo.

45 SELL YOUR OWN SAMPLES

Telling people about your brand can get them interested, but letting them experience it can win them over. The argument against is always going to be money. It's your financial manager's job to ask you to justify giving away free products free experiences in terms of the benefits they will see in increased sales. The answer to that is to test it, either by product or by location or by another measurable split, allowing one side to test your brand and the other side not to and keeping track of the results.

The idea

The perfume companies, who do give samples to customers when they launch a new fragrance, have come up with a good way to sell customers their samples. Both Penhaligon's and Ormonde Jayne do a small boxed set.

Penhaligon's set of samples comes in an elegant reusable tin rather like a cigar box. They are priced affordably so their potential customers can spend much less than the price of a single 50 ml bottle, and take their ten scents home with them to try over time and decide which they like before they splash out on their favourite.

The boxed sets also make a neat little present so happy customers will buy them and help to do your sampling for you.

In practice

- People are accustomed to being given samples for nothing, so in order to sell them and make customers feel good about your brand at the same time, your sample set should be attractive and of good value.
- If they are presented well enough, customers will buy your samples as gifts.
- You can also put an incentive voucher inside the box to encourage people to come back to visit.

46 SHAPE

Can someone recognise your product by its shape, even if they are too far away to read the label? There are good reasons to keep to the standard shapes, e.g. economies of scale, ease of packing and storage, and the list goes on. But being the same as everybody else isn't going to get you noticed. Owning a shape that is part of your brand identity might have more long-term benefits than saving on design and production costs.

The idea

The Coca Cola bottle is one of those great shapes. The Orangina bottle is also good, just not quite as famous. Of course they have to fit into cans too, to go into standard fridges and vending machines, but the original bottles make them stand out from their competition. The Pom pomegranate juice bottle is marvellous. It's shaped like three pomegranates sitting on top of each other. I will happily admit to buying that one because of the shape of the bottle.

Stockists are usually keen for you to package everything in rectangular boxes because they fit together with no space between them, using up less storage. Or perhaps you are not yet in a position to commission and manufacture your own designs. If that's the case, then you have to make your graphic design stand out instead.

But from the point of view of your brand, owning a shape that's such a part of your brand identity that everyone knows it you at first glance, might have more long-term value than saving on design and production costs.

In practice

- The aim is to make the shape of your product – or its packaging – distinctive so it draws people's attention without adding to the cost.

- Have a shape that adds to your brand values. There is no point in making something so distinctive that it just looks weird.

- Before you put a new design into production, check that it's just as effective as the previous one. There are stunningly designed teapots that pour tea all over the table rather than in the cups. Distinctive is only good if it is also useful.

47 SPECIALISE

When you are aiming to increase your turnover and a potential customers asks, "Can you do this?" It's tempting to think, "Hey, more business!" and reply, "We could do that, definitely!" While this might be a good chance for your organisation to grow, it can also distract you from your main purpose.

If you're going to make it clear to customer what makes you different from the rest, you need to have be clear about what's at the heart of your brand identity. One way to keep your focus is to be a specialist.

The idea

In the UK there is a shop called The Holding Company. It started in the King's Road, Chelsea and it's online too. It sells storage for your home and office. It's got one of those names with a dual meaning that makes you smile wrily: A holding company is one that owns others but doesn't do that much, but The Holding Company sells storage for your home and office. From soap dishes to shelving systems, baskets, vegetable racks, filing cabinets. Stuff that holds stuff. Things to help you keep tidy.

Their stock changes all the time, but their brand identity stays solid. They specialise in selling good quality storage tools for keeping the place tidy. Their founder even presented her own television programme on extreme decluttering, and they are regularly featured in the press.

In practice

- If you're a specialist then make this clear, with your name and in your publicity.

- Stay focused; you could sell other things, but that makes your identity fuzzy at the edges.

- Build partnerships with other brands who have similar customers, but mark your boundaries.

BE AN EXPERT

There is a difference between being a media spokesperson for your organisation, and appearing as an expert. As a spokesperson, you're generally invited on to the media when something bad has happened to your own organisation. Be prepared for that, but you can also volunteer your services as an expert to the media, to give your views on your area of expertise.

The idea

As a brand owner or guardian, you're not expected to be impartial. If you're invited to give an opinion to the press or to talk on the radio, they will always bear in mind that you have something you want to publicise. But if you can give good advice about your field, without showing a bias towards your own brand, the media will generally allow you the trade-off of mentioning your company.

If you do try to push your own brand, you won't get invited back, so there is a balance to observe.

You can also have media training. This is the professional version of practise videos, and teaches people how to come over well on television and radio, if they plan to be a spokesperson for their organisations. However, you can generally spot the media-trained. They refuse to answer questions and say, "That's not important, my point is..." Interviewers on news programmes loathe this and can be hostile to anyone who is defensive, closed and one-sided.

It's always refreshing to see experts answering questions openly rather than bulldozing their views through, and it builds the speaker's credibility.

In practice

- You can use an experienced PR company to advise you on how to present your brand, or you can go direct to the media and get advice on what they need.

- Some people are natural on television or radio, and some are walking disasters. To test your skills, do practice interviews and video them so you see how you come across.

- Tell the press about your in-house experts. Provide contact details and biographies if possible, so that the media can contact them if need be. Having expert views on talk shows and print material lends credibility to your brand.

- Send out press releases giving your expert view about stories that are in the news. It's a matter of building helpful relationships with the media. If you can help them to fill the pages or their allotted minutes with useful material, then you'll get a mention.

49 E-BRANDING 3: YOUTUBE

Even the BBC put their own trailers on YouTube, despite having their own channels and the BBC iPlayer. YouTube is an Internet resource where everyone can upload their own short films. If they are good, they can go viral. Meaning that people will send links to their friends urging them to watch, or post them on their Facebook pages, Twitter or other social media sites. It's a way to get your brand seen by people who don't usually watch television.

YouTube is now one of the world's biggest search engines. If you aren't there then you are missing an opportunity to be found and watched by millions of people.

The idea

If you have something to say about your brand, you can film it and upload it. If it's good, then it will be forwarded; if it's not that interesting it will fade away. There's a difference between buzz and hype; buzz is when people start to chat about your brand because they think it's worthwhile – because it's entertaining, amusing, useful, interesting or all those things. Hype is when you push too hard.

You can use YouTube to upload all your old advertisements, including the ones that were never released. Ford's banned SportKa "Evil Twin" ads did the rounds as people recommended them to their friends. Don't show them to animal lovers. They're not real, but they are quite evil. They were successful because they were very funny, in a twisted kind of way.

In practice

- Take a look at YouTube's top films to see what captures the imagination. Read the comments for the short clip to get a better idea.
- Look at what your competitors do. Then consider what you can upload to help build your brand identity.
- You can build your own YouTube channel, and brand it with your own colours, then host your own films there for your customers to see.

50 BRAND YOUR VEHICLES ...

Companies have always written their names on their names, ever since carriage-makers starting putting sides on to horse-drawn carts. If you make deliveries, or you travel around to meet your clients, take the opportunity to get your brand noticed.

As well as you name, you can add designs to the fabric sides of goods trailers, paint your logo on your railway trucks and personalise your pizza delivery bikes.

The idea

The London estate agents, Foxtons, have a fleet of Minis painted in green and yellow colours. You can't miss them. Some of their noticeable designs include hippie-flower patterns, some that look as if the passengers are being x-rayed, and sporty ones with big white circles.

Sandwich companies have their names on their delivery bicycles. Ice cream vans play their own music. Green organisations use electric vehicles, and even the new greener London red buses have "Big Green Bus" written on the sides to show their efforts to lower carbon emmissions in the city. The London Air Ambulance is bright red and has its sponsor's name painted on the sides of its rescue helicopter.

Innocent drinks started small, but with a talent for attracting attention. Their small vans are decorated with plastic grass to look like fields with for their fruit Smoothies or black and white with horns and a tail to look like cows for their yoghurt Thickies. They certainly get themselves spotted.

In practice

- If you've got to go to the expense of running your own vehicles, you might as well be noticed by the millions of people you pass by.
- Have vehicles that are an extension of your brand values. If you run a charity that helps to alleviate poverty, it would be a mistake to drive a branded Rolls Royce. But if you run a Rolls Royce dealership it would be shocking to see you in anything else.
- Keep close control of what goes on your vehicles. That includes bumper stickers and your drivers' personalisation, as well as your colours and logo.

51 ... AND DRIVE WELL

It's not just what you put on your company vehicles and the model you use that broadcasts your brand, it's how clean they are and how your drivers behave – the overall impression they give.

The idea

Drivers are respresenting your brand when they are out and about.

On London's North Circular Road recently, I saw a delivery van driven so badly that he skidded and swerved and only just avoided an accident in his hurry to get past car driving carefully, at 30 miles per hour above the speed limit, on the wrong side of him. The van belonged to a department store with a very good reputation for customer care and reliability, which its driver was doing his best to ruin.

As we mentioned, Innocent Drinks vans are dressed up as fields and cows, so there was no mistaking it when one of them came storming up my high street, again way over the speed limit, and didn't stop at the zebra crossing for me. I emailed them and told them all about it. They said sorry.

The company that is famous for putting its driving first is Eddie Stobart, the haulage and logistics business. Its staff always drive perfectly because their reputation for taking care of their customer's products depends on it. They are a textbook example of how to extend a brand identity into everyday behaviour.

In practice

- Adorning your vehicles with your brand identity is a great idea, but your values have got to extend to the drivers.
- Keep your vehicles clean, and your drivers behaviour squeaky clean.
- Encourage customers to report bad driving, to help control your brand identity.

E-BRANDING 4: EMAIL SIGNATURES

As long as people continue to send emails, inside the organisation as well as externally, there's a place for your brand identity on each one of them.

The idea

Your email signature is the bit that gets added to the bottom automatically each time you send out an email.

The best ones give contact details and show the company's strapline or logo. They'll also probably have a link to their website, and perhaps the company's Twitter feed and Facebook page too.

Some organisations' email signatures are obviously written by the legal department as there is a huge block of small disclaimer text explaining that if this email hashas gone to the wrong place then you must delete it and inform the sender immediately, and that all information contained in this email is confidential. No one reads it. Email signatures written in legalese make brands look boring and pompous, which can give the opposite impression from the one you want to give your customers. (Unless of course the email comes from a legal company.)

You can also make your "I'm away from my desk" emails

interesting to read. Take any opportunity you're offered to say something about your brand.

In practice

- You can change your organisation's email signature as often as you like, so if you have news, you can let everyone know it with a short line at the end of your emails.

- Sometimes organisations do get carried away and make their email signatures longer than the message. Others come across as rather boastful. Make sure yours matches your brand values.

53 THE BUILDING 1: RECREATING THE HISTORY

There are many reasons for a long-established organisation to move to a modern building out of town: Cost, maintenance, transport links, health and safety. Brand values don't always come into it. But when their brand identity is set firmly in the 19th or early 20th centuries to reflect their traditions, it's always a surprise to find them in a modern industrial unit. But there's no need to throw the baby out with the bathwater.

Even though they've left the old building, the interior of their new workplace can be designed to reflect a part of the brand's history.

The idea

Stepping inside a building and finding something completely different from what the exterior has led you to expect, can be a surprisingly pleasant experience.

Modern buildings don't have to be kitted out with plain white walls, light wood veneer office furniture and neutral carpet tiles. They can have floral wallpaper, antiques and polished floorboards, if that's what suits your brand best. Use your brand values to influence and inspire your building's interior. Of course it has to be functional but there's absolutely no need to make it into another identikit office.

All it takes is some imagination, interior design skills, and a clear understanding of your values.

In practice

- Ask your customers, the ones who have never visited, what they would your building to look like. Ask the ones who have visited if it was what they expected. You can begin to build a picture of the way your brand is seen from the outside.

- Get advice from an interior designer, tell them who you are and what you do, about your history and what your brand stands for, and ask for their interpretation.

- Of course you do need to comply with health and safety, but you can buy antique furniture at auctions that's a lot less expensive than modern office kit.

THE BUILDING 2: GO OUT

These days many people work from home. There are substantial organisations with no offices at all, so what happens when you meet the clients? You go out.

The idea

This is a story told in 1981 at an Advertising Association event for young trainees, by Lord Bell, the advertising man who described himself as "the ampersand between Saatchi & Saatchi". When his advertising agency first moved into their London offices, they had a huge, smart reception area with comfortable chairs for the clients. Everyone else in the whole team was packed into one room behind it.

When clients visited, Tim Bell said that he and the team would arrange to meet at midday and sweep them straight out for lunch, after giving them the impression that they had an equally swish office behind the door that led from the reception area. For a big meeting, the team would generously offer to travel to the clients' offices.

Once the agency could afford to expand they took more space, and started to invite clients into their own building, which, by that time, was as large and luxurious as the clients had always imagined.

To avoid the dissonance between their brand values and the facts, Saatchi & Saatchi carefully managed the situation until the two sides reflected each other perfectly. They pulled it off so well because in their hearts they knew that was the kind of agency they were really going to be.

In practice

- When your building doesn't yet match your aspirations, hold your meetings somewhere that does.
- If you work from home, and you don't feel comfortable holding meetings there, volunteer to travel to the client's place, hire a hotel meeting room or a use a company that rents out office facilities.
- The occasional lunch treat is cheaper than the rent for a building, so balance out your costs before you decide to move into a more expensive space.

THE BUILDING 3:
A CAREFUL COPY

When you go to the trouble of creating something that looks sufficiently like the real thing, customers will generally except it as authentic. And if your brand dates back over 300 years it's unlikely that anyone will question your right to a historical brand identity. The difficulty comes when you want to change it.

The idea

In the 1990s and 2000s, department stores were bringing light and life back into their buildings by knocking huge holes down the centre, putting in staircases or escalators, giving a pleasant feeling of space and air.

In 2007, Fortnum & Mason did the same thing, in the year of their 300th anniversary. They had complaints from customers who were shocked at their destruction of what their issues to be an original Georgian building. Fortnum & Mason wrote back and their customers were astonished to find that the current Fortnum & Mason building was constructed in neo-Georgian style in the 1920s, and that the clock attached to the front, over the Piccadilly entrance, was added in the 1950s by its American owner, is a tribute to the original grocers.

The 21st-century remodelling was one more step in the gentle restyling of Fortnum & Mason which had gradually been taking place over 300 years. They kept their traditional look by placing an elegant staircase from the basement to the top. In 20 years time customers will have forgotten the remodelling, and will assume the staircase is original.

In practice

- A company with a traditional brand identity and a conservatively minded clientele must tread carefully when making radical changes.
- Facsimiles will be accepted as authentic, as long as they sit perfectly within the brand identity.
- Don't let traditional values hold back changes that the desirable and necessary; handle them well.

HOP ON THE BANDWAGON

We've all heard about jumping on the bandwagon but the whole phrase goes like this: We can all jump on the bandwagon, but we can't all play the tune.

The idea

Playing the tune is the domain of the innovators. They take the risks and stand to take advantage of being first in the field, but they also take on the responsibility of introducing a new idea. It might succeed, but it might just as easily fail.

The art of jumping on the bandwagon is to be there just behind the band, once you are sure that they are playing a tune people will dance to. But enough of the music metaphors, let's look at the branding.

There are times when the innovators are putting so much energy into breaking new ground, that the followers are in a better position to make their own brands a success; they don't need to educate the market, because that's been done. It's a question of timing, and also of intellectual property rights.

In the fashion industry almost anything goes, and that includes copying other people's designs. The market moves so quickly, with new fashion collections coming out twice a year, in Paris, Milan, London and New York, that the intellectual property laws can hardly keep up with it, and often brands decide that their resources are better spent on coming up with new ideas than going to court and expensively protecting old ones.

Whether you consider this to be ethical or not, it still happens. People can buy cheaper copies of designer brands at the disposable fashion end of the market. Sir Philip Green, owner of Top Shop and other high street retailers, explained to the press that he invigorated the chain by buying Paris designer clothes, taking them back to the UK, unpicking them, having them copied and manufactured and selling them in his own shops.

Some high street retailers claim that this is a quest for fairness, that they are the Robin Hoods of the fashion industry bringing style to people who can't afford the originals. But that's mostly codswallop. It's more about profiting from copying other people's designs without the expense of employing designers or the risk of breaking new ground.

However, there are ways to follow trends legally, and to move into a market as it expands. The innovators don't necessarily want to fulfil the entire market demand. Their brand identity places them at the cutting edge, so they will have moved on by the time the followers are ready to adopt their ideas.

In practice

- Keep a close eye on innovation from brands in your industry.
- If there's something that will appeal to your customers and that you can adopt or adapt legally, consider marrying that idea with your current brand identity.
- Perhaps you can improve upon the original, take the idea and make it even more successful. You might be able to copyright or patent your improvements.

GO WHERE THE ACTION IS

There is a classic piece of retail advice: If you want to open a shoe shop, open it next to the other shoe shop.

You might think that it's best to go somewhere completely new, somewhere that doesn't already have what you are offering. But in the words of the extremely successful strategic operator, Rupert Murdoch, "There might be a gap in the market, but is there a market in the gap?" He said this about Sir James Goldsmith's failed news magazine, Now!, in answer to Goldsmith's persistent claims that the UK was ready and waiting for his great idea.

Sometimes there is a gap in the market, but often there is no demand at all. If there are a couple of successful shoe shops in a street, then that's where people are going to buy shoes.

The idea

Places have reputations for specialising trades or products. This can date back several hundred years to times when businesses will conveniently located by a railway station, or the port, or in the case of London, granted the rights to practice certain trades in a specific location. Ealing, West London, became the centre of the UK's perfume industry, dating from the time that William Perkin synthesised the first copy of a natural scent molecule, courmarin, at his Greenford works in the 1860s.

In London, Harley Street is the place where you expect to find medical specialists. However all you need to practise there is the money for the rent, not a medical qualification. Senior consultants with private practices are still found there, but so are many other people who wish to bask in the reflected glory that comes from the Harley Street brand identity.

In practice

- Location is part of your brand positioning, literally and figuratively. Physically placing yourself at the heart of your industry will add credibility to your brand.
- If you do position yourself geographically amongst your competitors, be clear about how you are going to position your brand differently.
- Bring something new and better, so that your brand gives people an extra reason to visit the area not just more of the same.

The nature of your brand can dictate the kind of building that you need for your business. If people are prepared to travel to you, wherever you're based, then your location is less important than the space and structure you need.

The idea

The Sarva Iyengar Yoga Institute is led by Sheila Haswell and her business partner Ally Hill. As yoga teachers they set up a business and travelled with cars and trailers carrying their equipment from class to class. They used village halls, church halls, schools and even a modern church building. In the meantime, they were searching for a suitable place to conduct their yoga classes. Their need for the right building, which had the right facilities and the right atmosphere for the Sarva yoga brand, was more important than the location.

They found the perfect place, a former factory built in the 1930s, a light airy space with lots of windows, wooden floors, a large car park for visiting students, and space for an eating area, changing rooms, offices and rooms for therapy sessions. It was set back from the main road heading out of town, and difficult to spot if you didn't know exactly where you are heading.

Sheila and Ally had a simple but effective solution. They printed their logo on purple flags and put them up the flagpoles where they could be seen from the road. New visitors driving along the long straight road could spot Sarva early enough to indicate, slow down and turning through the narrow gate.

It's a sign that clearly but gently says, "We're here!"

In practice

- Of course we can look things up on Google maps, and use StreetView to look at the building online, but a branded flag in a corporate colour is easy to spot in real life.
- Flags symbolise celebration, as well as territory. They're an inexpensive, underused addition to the branding toolkit.
- You need permission to put up a flagpole, and a branded flag is regarded as advertising so before you fly one check with your local council.

BE PART OF THE EXPERIENCE

There are things that people buy in certain places that they would never consider buying anywhere else. Popcorn at the cinema, Kendal Mint Cake while walking in the Lake District, ice cream during the interval at the theatre, strawberries and cream at Wimbledon. It's not just food; we like to buy souvenirs that remind us of an experience and that we associate with geographical areas or features.

The idea

Take the seaside, for example. Falmouth in Cornwall, on the south western tip of Great Britain has a maritime tradition going back hundreds and probably thousands of years. On Falmouth high street there are shops selling Cornish pasties, boxes of fudge, sailing clothes and sea salt.

You'll also find a branch of Seasalt, a Cornish company which sells stripy clothing designed for wearing at the seaside, particularly the British seaside where you can expect some, rain, wind and the occasional calm spell usually all in one day. You can wear Seasalt's clothes and shoes and carry their canvas beach bags in the city, but it's more likely that you'd want to buy them where you can taste the salt in the air.

Their strapline, "Designed by the sea for people everywhere", sums it up nicely.

They make striped shirts and sweaters, windproof and rainproof clothing, things that are ideal for pulling over your swimsuit at the end of a day on the beach. They sell a week's worth of stripy sailors' socks in a gift box for you to take home for yourself or the cat-sitter.

Their window displays, with old maps and battered antique suitcases, combine nostalgia and happiness, reminding us of childhood holidays on British beaches.

Their brand identity succeeds because they've made such a good job of bringing our memories up-to-date, and they make such great clothes, and they are in exactly the right place.

In practice

- What's your area known for? Can your brand identity take advantage of your location?
- Seasalt succeeds because their designs and manufacture quality are good enough to make the journey back into the city. (Unlike so many things that we bring back from our holidays and wonder if we've taken leave of our senses once we're home.) You've got to be more than a mere souvenir.
- For the brand to ring true, it's got to be authentic.

PICK A COLOUR

The human eye can spot hundreds of shades and depth of colour, but realistically we can only distinguish between a generous handful of them unless they're placed right next to each other.

The idea

Choose a distinctive colour for your brand.

In the 1980s, when tobacco advertising was still allowed, Silk Cut, a brand of low-tar cigarettes, was launched with teaser ads using photographs of ripped pieces of purple silk, but no words. Casual observers assumed that they were for Cadbury's dairy milk chocolate which was the best-known purple brand around, unless they looked closely at the health warning, which was smaller in those days.

It was a surprise when the cigarettes were launched; the pack never appeared on the consumer ads, just in the press trade. Silk Cut's purple and white packaging certainly stood out on the shelves compared with the other cigarette brands of the time, which were in combinations of black, red, blue, white and gold. The imagery was questionable. At a time when people were becoming more aware of the damage that smoking does to health, photographs of silk with scalpel cuts, needles and what looked like surgical scissors were perhaps not the most reassuring images. All the same, it was said to be the most successful cigarette launch ever.

Silk cut purple turned out to be slightly more red than Cadbury's purple but no one would know that unless they were trained designers or could see the two of them sitting next to each other on poster billboards. So while the Cadbury purple is still the strongest claim on the colour, Silk Cut took it into another market and made it their own. Among smokers if someone offers you a cigarette from a white and purple pack, no one's going to say, "What's that then?" Among non-smokers, it'll probably want to make them buy chocolate.

In practice

- Stick with the colour you have chosen.
- Avoid colour swhich used by big organisations in your own market; even if they haven't been able to trademark it, you will only help to build their brands not your own.
- Use it conspicuously, but not to the point of obliterating your own message.

BEEN THERE, DONE THAT ...

And now, sell the T-shirt. T-shirts, like carrier bags, are And now, sell the T-shirt. T-shirts, like carrier bags, are walking billboards. If your designs are good enough and people like your brand, then they are happy to advertise for you on their fronts and backs. T-shirts are great souvenirs of an experience or a place, mostly because they're so useful. People wear them, even if it's under their shirts (which is how they started out, as underwear), to do the gardening or to sleep in. And most of us wear them for work or play a few times a week.

The idea

Buying a T-shirt as a reminder of an experience has become such a habit that it's even inspired satirical (if clichéd) T-shirts of its own: "Been there, done that, got the T-shirt" and "My parents went to London and all I got was this lousy T-shirt" – available in many variations.

London Transport will always concentrate on its main purpose, that of moving people around the capital, but they also keep a watchful eye on their intellectual property. Companies cannot use the London Underground map, or their roundel logo, or any variation on them without a license or their permission.

They also realised that a trip to London usually includes at least one ride on a bus, tube, boat or now a London Underground bicycle. And with the London Underground Museum right bang slap in the middle of Covent Garden tourist central, they are well set to take advantage of merchandising their brand.

My personal favourites are the bags made from the leftover rolls of bus and tube seat fabric. I've one made from the former Northern Line fabric. Greetings cards use the artwork from historic London Underground posters are beautiful too. All those things spread the transport network brand identity way beyond London's limits, including the very popular "Mind The Gap" T-shirts.

In practice

- Selling merchandise can strengthen your brand position and make your customers happy, but make sure that it doesn't distract you from running your main business.
- People like to support events and organisations that they admire. You can produce your own, or license your brand to specialists, like toy manufacturers or publishers.
- If there's a market for it, you can also sell your branded merchandise through other outlets, and online.

ADD TO THE ATMOSPHERE

We tend to think that a great atmosphere is down to a mixture of indefinable things that just magically fit together to create a fortunate situation. It's the people, the lighting, the music ... but you can't make it happen. The scientists would argue otherwise.

The idea

Professor Charles Spence is a neursoscientist who runs the Crossmodal Research Laboratory at Oxford University's Department of Experimental Psychology. His work explores the way our senses react with each other to influence the way we think, and shows that we are influenced in different ways from the rational ones we're aware of.

For example, he has shown that if underarm deodorant external packaging is rough, we think that the deodorant itself feels uncomfortable. If the same deodorant has smooth packaging, we believe it feels fine.

We think we prefer one crisp to another because of the taste, but the most important element turns out to be the crunch it makes as we bite it.

We've all heard about the theory about how brewing coffee when potential buyers come round can make it easier to sell your house, and how supermarkets use the synthetic fragrance of freshly baked bread to attract people into their shops.

Professor Spence's work also includes the effect of adding

different sensory experiences to create pleasant sensations within a shopping centre. To summarise and simplfy, he has discovered that there's a balance; you can add a certain number of sensory stimuli, including music, lighting and scent, and people will be attracted into a shop or a mall and stay longer. If you overdo it, they all leave.

In practice

- Multinationals are commissioning Professor Spence's department and similar scientific institutions to research the perfect combination of scent, sound, light, touch, taste and other senses that aren't usually mentioned, to build their brands' ideal ambiance.
- Notice when you go somewhere that feels just right. Stop and analyse what it's they are doing. Experiment with your own space.
- If you do add a sensory stimulus, choose something that complements your brand.

63 | BE FRIENDLY

One great way to build a relationship between your brand and your customers is to show that you really are who you say you are, and have real people answer the phone. The trend is towards automated systems, making it more and more difficult to reach a real person. This might save money, but the jury's out on how many customers it annoys and loses along the way.

As customers, we all want to be heard and helped out. Even if the organisation can't solve a problem, marketing research has shown that giving people the opportunity to air their views, and to get an answer, helps to keep your customers, rather than encouraging them to look somewhere else for better service.

The idea

First Direct is a UK bank that started as a telephone only service, a branch of the Midland (now HSBC). They made a promise that there would always be a person to answer the phone. Occasionally there's a short wait but that is the rare exception. You can have a person tell you what's happening with your account every hour of the day, every day of the year, including high days and holidays.

They were also quick to set up online banking, rightly predicting that people who wanted to do their personal banking at the exact moment they chose would also want the same service and more online.

But unlike some companies who used to switch to online support to discourage customers from calling them, First Direct have kept the service, keeping their reputation as a friendly, personal service despite being part of a massive multinational bank.

In practice

- When customers call they have a reason, a question to be answered. The faster you solve their problems, the faster they will return to being satisfied customers.

- Put yourself in your customers' shoes. If your service doesn't come up to the standard you would expect, then you are damaging your brand. Employ good people and give your brand a friendly and personable face.

- Publish your phone number and answer it when it rings. A quick conversation can sort out issues faster than a series of letters or emails.

GET A GRAN IN

The modern obsession with the young and beautiful can be counterproductive for brands. There are hotels and shops who deliberately – and illegally – recruit people on the basis of their looks, but as that's difficult to prove, it still goes on, despite well known organisations being taken to employment tribunals.

The belief that young, beautiful staff make your brand more attractive is often misplaced.

The idea

In the 1980s, an airline announced that it was going to be retiring its female air crew early; they had decided that their mostly male businesses passengers only wanted to be taken care of by younger women. They wanted to reposition their brand with the help of young, glamorous, sexy air hostesses, as they were still called. This was greeted by a fair amount of outrage in the press. What the airline staff weren't expecting was that their male passengers started asking for the older crew members to be brought back again. Some of the staff who had been retired were asked to come back.

Delta Airlines also make their business class customers feel at home by putting their most senior, experienced staff at their service on long haul flights.

It was a case of image being trumped by effectiveness. One of the reasons that business people travelled with the airline was they got a quiet, efficient service. They wanted to be given their meals and drinks by responsible considerate people, and be allowed to travel in peace. Neither women nor men wanted the attention of young women who'd been sent to charm them and amuse them.

Boldon, Tyne & Wear, is probably best known for the occasional mention by the comedian Sarah Millican, who's been known to shop at the Asda. Boldon's big supermarket has the most marvellous greeters you could hope for. They turn grocery shopping from an everyday, slightly tedious chore, into a happy occasion. Their managers have recruited grandmothers to give everyone a cheery Geordie hello as customers come in the front door, and help them find what they need.

Organisations pontificate about diversity, including employing older people, but often there is an unspoken feeling that they want to put the young ones at the front and hide the older ones inside the warehouse. They could help to build their brands' reputations for helpfulness and effectiveness by putting people with experience and wisdom on the front line.

In practice

- To learn more about how older staff can contribute to your organisation, read *The Secret Life of the Grown-Up Brain* by Barbara Strauss.
- Older people often take things in their stride that younger people don't know how to deal with. They've seen it all before. A balance of young enthusiasm and energy with older experience and wisdom will give you a stronger team.
- Recruit people who behave well towards your customers,

65 E-BRANDING 5: CUT THE FAQs

We're all individuals, as the Monty Python team reminded us. When we have a question, it's our question and we want an individual answer. Maybe a thousand people have asked it before, but it's still irritating to visit a website, click the "contact us" button and get redirected to a page that says "check here first to see if it answers your question". It rarely does, and even if we do find an answer, it makes us feel as if we've been fobbed off.

The idea

FAQs, frequently asked questions, were an early feature of websites, and in the 1990s they were quite helpful. They were designed to help first-timers to understand how the website work. Since then they have been expanded on some sites, in an attempt to answer every question that a customer could possibly ask. The expense put into creating these massive, interactive FAQ sections must have been huge, and yet when you come to the box at the end that says "Did this answer your question", the answer is generally, "Well, not really, no."

Replacing people with FAQs puts a barrier between your brand and your customers, something which is likely to send them off in another direction.

Innocent drinks have a banana phone. They really do, and it's shaped like a banana. You can call it at any time and talk to someone who works there. They also invite you to drop into their offices for a chat. You really can. And if you email them, you get an answer.

In practice

- The fewer mistakes you make, the less likely you are to get complaints. If you're dealing with too many customers calling to report faults and errors, the answer is not to hide the contact details and direct customers to the FAQ section, it's to fix the problems. The problems are damaging your brand, and FAQs won't help.

- Train your people to listen to problems and offer solutions.

- A small percentage of people enjoy complaining on principle. True, they can be a massive pain. But most people hate to complain. Encourage your customers to report anything wrong, like they would report a gas leak, helpfully. Thank them, act on it and your brand will have their support.

66 TRY THE NPS

When filling in research questionnaires, people are notoriously positive about their own behaviour. I say notoriously, because some organisations have found themselves on the rocks after failing to question high scores as an accurate prediction of their product's future success.

One of my marketing students ran a research project for a tobacco company in Eastern Europe when the countries were still part of the Communist bloc. They asked smokers which brands they bought. The results said that more people smoked one particular western brand than they had ever sold cigarettes in that country, even accounting for grey imports. The research respondents had liked to think of themselves as the kind of people who would smoke that brand, if only they could get hold of it, so they ticked "yes".

Then there's the tendency to give a higher score just to be kind. When people answer "how likely are you to buy our toothpaste?" with a 7 out of 10, that does not mean they are 70% likely to do it; it means they probably won't touch it, but they didn't want to be rude.

The idea

NPS stands for Net Promoter Score. it's an ingenious (trademarked) way to found out what people really think of your brand, developed by Fred Reichheld and described in his book *The Ultimate Question*.

The question is: How likely are you to recommend us to a friend or colleague?

Reichheld worked out that asking people if they would recommend it was more likely to get a straight answer, that 7 or 8 out of ten are " Passive or Neutral" and that 0 to 6 are negative, "Detractors". Only a 9 or a 10 is a positive answer, "Promotors". Your NPS is your positive score, minus your negative score.

NPS has been adopted as a method to find out the answer to the one big question: How do your customers feel about your brand?

There is a debate about what the answer means and about whether it can predict what to do next. One really useful thing to measure is if it goes up or down over time.

In practice

- It's a great place to start.
- Using the NPS will give you an idea of how much work you have to do on improving your branding before your customers will recommend you.
- If you get a good result, then you're doing something right, but don't rest on your laurels, do more of it. You might still want to follow up on the reasons behind the negatives. If you get a bad result, look into deeper ways to identify the issues.

67 E-BRANDING 6: TWITTER

Twitter is one of the most successful social media. Each "tweet" is a message of 140 characters or less. Tweeting is becoming an art form; some writers specialise in writing short, interesting sentences in their own or their brand's tone of voice. It's instant. People will tweet from wherever they are using their phones or their laptops.

Consider your Twitter identity as part of your brand. If you aren't there, you're missing an opportunity.

The idea

Do you need to be there? You need to take a look at it, and see what your competitors are doing to find out. But, generally speaking, yes you do. You're expected to be there, in the same way as you are expected to have a website, a blog, or both.

Using Twitter you can link to interesting sites including your own, to films, photographs or anything else on the Internet. You can use it for research to find out what other people are tweeting about, including your competitors. You can post useful information. If you write or link to something interesting, people will pass them on by "retweeting" them to their own followers.

If you use it badly, just for blowing your own trumpet and telling customers how marvellous you are, it will work against you. Allow your brand to show its human side, and Twitter will work for you. It's an extra way to build up a direct relationship between your brand and the outside world. If you're small you can get away with tweeting once a day, and replying to direct messages from customers. You really do have to reply to all your messages, so if you aren't prepared to do that yet, don't build yourself a presence.

In practice

- You can use Twitter to build your brand, and as a way to search for mentions, good or bad.
- Twitter can be a dreadful place for gossip. People are happy to spread rumours there without finding out first whether or not they are true. The sooner you find something tweeted about you that's not good, you can answer it directly, and nip any nastiness in the bud.
- You will attract followers by being useful, informative, funny, interesting or just by being famous and popular.

E-BRANDING 7: FACEBOOK

At the time of writing, Facebook has millions of users around the globe and Linked In is a professional network, which people use for business contacts. Google+ is at the beta testing stage, so even though we're using it we can't quite tell if it's going to take over the world, but it looks set to combine the benefits of both, as well as integrating itself with Google's many other components.

For the moment, let's look at Facebook. It started as the online version of a college yearbook. Now it's much more than that, and although parents might think it's just for teenagers to waste their time and they ought to be doing their homework, many businesses are using it successfully to be "friends" with their customers.

The idea

Individuals and organisations can have their own pages on Facebook. To make a success of it, you need your page to be "liked", not just in the abstract sense, but that your Facebook friends have to click the "like" button to show that they really mean it.

You get well-known on Facebook by being liked, because each time somebody clicks on your like button, because you've written or shared something that amuses them, their friends will be able to see it too.

Marmite is one of the brands which uses Facebook well. Each time you see a Marmite status update arrive in your Facebook timeline you know it's going to be worth reading. They have competitions, surveys, they ask their customers' opinions, share Marmite recipes and sometimes just chat to you about how they're getting along. As a brand, Marmite - with its love/hate relationship with the world, instantly recognisable bottle and logo, and the series of cheeky ads it's been running over the last decade – is just right for Facebook and has taken full advantage of the opportunity to build its brand there.

In practice

- Be friendly. There's no place here for corporate claptrap or brand hype.
- Just like Twitter, the brand guardians you put in charge of your Facebook presence must be able to write succinctly in your brand style.
- It's social media; you've got to be interactive. People will post comments about your status updates so be prepared to reply openly to them.

MASCOT

69

Some brands have something that no one else does. We're not talking about that certain something in their personality; we're talking about an actual physical feature, probably trademarked.

It's one of those effective parts of a brand identity that people recognise and say immediately, "I know that, it's a..." and can give you the brand name.

The idea

Rolls Royce has the Spirit of Ecstasy, designed by Charles Robinson Sykes and used from 1911. Car emblems which stuck up from the bonnet, like Jaguar's jaguar and Mercedes' roundel, were banned for safety reasons, but allowed back as long as they can retract instantly. They were such an important part of brand identity that some car manufacturers went developed the technology necessary the technology to get their emblems back.

The Spirit of Ecstasy wasn't an oringal Rolls Royce feature. The fashion was to have your own emblem made to personalise your vehicle. Lord Montagu of Beaulieu, John Walter Edward Douglas-Scott-Montagu, asked his friend Sykes, recently graduated from London's Royal College of Art to design his mascot, and it's believed to have been modelled on his secretary, mistress and love of his life, Eleanor Velasco Thornton.

Charles Sykes described it as "a graceful little goddess, the Spirit of Ecstasy, who has selected road travel as her supreme delight and alighted on the prow of a Rolls-Royce motor car to revel in the freshness of the air and the musical sound of her fluttering draperies."

When Rolls Royce noticed that some personal mascots did not reflect their vision of their beautiful vehicles, they commissioned Sykes to manufacture the Spirit of Ecstasy for them.

Now it's 100 years old and a huge part of their brand identity. At times designers must have been tempted to modernise it, but apart from a smaller version for sports cars and the US "Flying Lady" it stays the same.

In practice

- Here's an example of a great brand idea that came from a customer. Enthusiastic supporters of your brand sometimes know its details and history even better than the staff. Take advantage of their passion, and encourage them to share their ideas.
- Not changing can be a more courageous decision than modernising.
- Changes in safety regulations inspired creative engineering to preserve Rolls Royce's, Jaguar's and Mercedes best-known brand features. Don't let health and safety defeat you.

70

SPONSOR A TEAM

This could be a risky strategy, because the ardent fans of your team's greatest rivals will refuse to give you their business, but on the other hand you have the loyal support of your own.

There are different levels of sponsorship, and different sizes of team. Some get regular TV coverage and others are likely to get 100 supporters to watch a home game. Choose one to match your aims and your budget in a sport that really interests you so you can enjoy supporting them. For local businesses it's a great brand idea.

The idea

At the risk of offending the rest of the English football league, let's consider Arsenal, known to its lifelong supporters as "The Arsenal", originally named after the Woolwich Arsenal in south London where they started playing. They crossed the river in 1913 and even had a London Underground station named after the team.

In 2006 Arsenal left their old stadium for the new one, the Emirates; everyone going in and out of King's Cross railway station can see the stadium with its huge red logo on the side. Emirates and Arsenal might not seem like an obvious pairing at first, unless you consider the number of holidays that premiership footballers take in Dubai.

Perhaps the most noticeable part of the Emirates' sponsorship – at least for non-football fans – is the stadium itself. Traditionally, football grounds were named after their location, like Trafford Park or Stamford Bridge. My own team played at Ayresome Park for decades then when they moved to the new modern stadium by the River Tees old docks, they named it the Riverside. Naming the whole ground after a sponsor is a recent development.

In practice

- Choose a team that operates in your geographical area, whether that's just along your street, throughout the country or internationally.
- Talk to the team about your options. Is there something they need that you can support, and perhaps get press coverage for doing so?
- Take full advantage. Mention your sponsorship on your own materials, include space in the match programmes for your advertising, exchange links on your websites.

HAVE A CATCHPHRASE

The tricky thing about catchphrases is you never know if they're going to catch on until you give it a try.

Comedians are the people who've traditionally made the most of catchphrases to establish their professional identities, sometimes by good luck rather than planning because when they stick, they stick. Sir Bruce Forsyth has his "Nice to see you. To see you, nice." which is now into its sixth decade. The Fast Show team created a comedy series based almost entirely on catchphrases from the jazz clubs "Mmmm... Nice!" To Arabella Weir's "does my bum look big in this?"

The way to make them catch on is repetition, and reaching a wider audience.

The idea

Specsavers is a chain of opticians that has always positioned itself as a brand that gives good value, with two pairs for the price of one.

Their television ads have always been amusing. For several years they featured their two-for-the-price-of-one deal. Then they changed. Picture a beautifully shot black-and-white film with a lone, ancient shepherd rounding up his sheep for shearing with the help of his faithful dog. Then we see the dog with his fur shaved off, then the shepherd's face with an unfocused look in his eyes and we hear the line:

"Should have gone to Specsavers."

They still used the same catchphrase, but it started to mean more to people when it was used to point out mistakes people make when they can't see what they're doing, instead of just how to save money. What's great about it is that it applies so often to everyday life, and that it has the brand name in it.

Ronseal have registered "Does exactly what it says on the tin®". This catchphrase has also moved into everyday life, but unfortunately it doesn't mention Ronseal.

In practice

- If it's funny enough, any ad with a catchphrase will be on YouTube before you know it and it'll go viral. Put yours there yourself.
- See if you can get your brand name into your catchphrase.
- It might take a few goes before you get one that actually catches on.

GET IT RIGHT AND NO-ONE NOTICES

When you get your spelling, grammar and punctuation right, it makes your writing easier to read, but no-one really notices that. They just read what you've written. That's why it's important to put your apostrophes in the right place. The people who believe that these details are very important will be happy and the people who don't know the difference won't be bothered either way.

The idea

An experienced training director once explained to me the way in which small details affect a brand identity. She said that when you're on an aeroplane and you're given a coaster with a coffee stain on it, you think the plane might fall out of the sky. It gives the impression that people don't care about details. If they don't care about the coasters, perhaps they've forgotten to oil the ailerons. When you're given a clean coaster, it's just a coaster and it doesn't disturb your train of thought.

When you're writing for business, your aim is to get people interested so that they start reading, keep them interested until they get to the end, then encourage them to do something. That could be anything from buying a house to changing their views. If you distract them by making your writing difficult to follow, then you'll distract them and lose their attention.

In practice

- There are plenty of people who love proofreading; they like nothing better than to spot your errors and point them out to you. Bring it on. Better that they're spotted and corrected by your own people than your customers.

- Although there is no grammar book, not even Gower, that says you can't start a sentence with and or but, there are millions of people who were taught this at school. If you are dealing with people who were taught by grammarians with Victorian values, don't do it, because it upsets them.

- Ad copy is different. Short sentences. They love it. But that's a particular style that belongs in headlines and on poster sites. Leave it out of your web copy and your customer letters.

E-BRANDING 8: SEARCH ENGINES

Search engine optimisation (SEO) aims to get your website to appear high up on the front page of Google and other search engine sites. Each search engine has an algorithm, a list of rules it uses to decide who gets promoted and who gets dropped. It's better for your brand to be towards the top of the list, so it's good to know what will help you get there.

Beware SEO specialists who try to change your brand's writing style to "optimise" your text. You can still write in an interesting way and use their other skills to boost your search engine rankings.

The idea

Search engines' customers are their users. A search engine must keep its customers happy so they continue to use it, rather than a different one. A search engine's brand identity is based on its ability to find what you're looking for. So the job of a search engine algorithm is to find websites they think their users will want hello and put them at the top of the list.

If your website is updated regularly, then search engines make the reasonable assumption that they are more interesting than those which never change. So if you have a blog on your website and you add to it each day or every week, or you post your tweets from Twitter straight onto your website, or have customer comments pages so other people or updating your website for you, this will help you get a leg up the search engine ladder.

LOCALISATION

Do your brand values translate into other cultures? Localisation experts check that they do. Localisation includes translation, but it's much more than that. We've all read translations that have been done on the cheap, word for word, without taking into account any of the deeper cultural meanings or stories behind the stories. Localisation takes a basic translation, puts it into fluent mother tongue, and checks that the references are appropriate, or changes the ones which aren't.

The idea

When I working was with Lush, based on Poole, on England's south coat, they brought out a Mothers Day gift called Mum, and the northerners amongst the creative team begged for a local version called Mam. Because it would sell better. In America they call theirs Mom.

Our Canadian colleagues wrote that we could take our Lush solid shampoo with us "to the lake in summer". The British adapted that "to the beach on holiday".

There's an infamous localisation story which circulated around the advertising industry. It concerned a brand of baby food, which came packed in tins with pictures of smiling happy babies on the labels. The UK advertising industry had moved over to depicting the benefits of their products rather than the features.

In Africa, the baby food wasn't selling. It turned out that the local languages didn't all exist in a written form, so the tradition was to show the contents of the tin instead. Result: One huge misunderstanding, that Europeans ate babies. Generally, localisation issues aren't quite this dramatic, but mistakes can make you look a bit silly. Obviously this is bad for your brand.

In practice

- When you venture into new territory, even if it's only as far as County Durham is from Dorset, check that what you're saying about your brand means the same thing to a different market.

- Translation isn't good enough when you're taking your words from your own language into a new one. Use localisation too.

- Your basic brand values will probably translate more easily into a new culture than everything you say about them, and the local brand stories you tell. Make sure that you get your values across, then encourage your new partners to create their own material.

75 MUSIC

Music is an amazing way to create an emotional response. You probably have a clear idea already of the kind of music that fits your own brand. Advertising has always use music, ever since radio and television commercials were first produced but often they wrote their own jingles. They used classical music too.

The idea

But it all changed when the UK ad agency, Bartle Bogle Hegarty, made their Launderette commercial for Levi's. We heard Marvin Gaye's "Heard it Through the Grapevine" as Nick Kamen took off his jeans and sat in his perfect white underwear while his Levi's went round and round in the washing machine.

By the 90s you could watch the whole commercial break and only hear songs. There was no dialogue, only atmosphere and action. And the atmosphere was supplied by the music. If you are choosing a tune for your advertising, pick something that isn't associated with another brand already. So many brands use The Gotan Project's modern interpretation of Argentinean tango music that it's become generic. Whereas if you hear Sugarbabes' version of "Here come the girls" it makes you want to march straight into Boots the Chemist.

Not all brands advertise, but in your shop, restaurant or while waiting for someone at the call centre to answer the phone, music changes the atmosphere. Loud music in a place people go to talk is annoying, but in a place people go to dance is perfect.

The type of music you pick also attracts different kinds of customers.

In practice

- Music helps an empty space to feel less intimidating, but choose the right style something to match your brand identity. A mismatch will be inconsistent and customers will feel that there is something not quite right.
- Balance your music with other sensory inputs; if you overload people they'll leave. And don't whack the volume up to 11.
- Register with the Performing Rights Society, and visit their website to check the law www.PRSformusic.com before you play music on your premises.

76 DISTINCTIVE DESIGNS

Great graphic designers think of new ways to arrange lines and colours in a manner that the rest of us can't. They can make a new approach stand out from the others in ways that people can see but can be very difficult to trademark. In fashion and other design led industries, a recognisable design, even if it's not a trademark, will give a brand it's clear point of difference.

The idea

Orla Kiely is a designer who has a way of working simple, geometric, floral and leaf designs in a small combination of plain colours so that they stand out as undisputedly hers, even without putting logos on them. After designing for other people, she and her husband set up their own business using her designs to build a distinctive brand.

A friend of mine handmakes her own bags and bought a remnant of material, waterproof fabric designed for outdoor tablecloths, with a geometric spotty design on it. She made it up into a shopping bag and was most annoyed when people kept asking her "Is that an Orla Kiely?"

Orla Kiely's combination of bright, simple designs made up into good quality products, priced at the top end of midmarket, have helped her to create a successful international brand in less than two decades.

In practice

- Great design can inspire a whole brand. IF yours is feeling jaded, invite a designer in.

- Visit the final year shows at art colleges to spot talented new designers.

- Protect your designs as well as you can legally, but bear in mind that if you're copied it's because you've led the way. Move on, and build a brand on leading the way.

77 E-BRANDING 9: YOUR OWN BLOG

Customers expect to find information about your organisation on your website. Put it there for them to find. If you have regular news to share, you might find that the best way to do this is to start a blog.

Blogs, short for web logs, are Internet-based diaries where you can update customers and anyone else who is interested. Your blog will become the place people go to for the latest information.

The idea

Your organisation can have one or several blogs, depending on how much you have to tell. Your writers must stick to your brand's tone of voice in your posts but they can adapt to suit the audience their writing for. There are blogs for the press, on environmental improvements, new products, sourcing, research and other areas that interest both staff and customers, and all the other people your organisation interacts with.

Blogs keep your customers up-to-date, give them a good reason to stay in touch with you and the opportunity to encourage them to get involved. They also help you to climb your way up the search engine rankings.

In practice

- Open up your blogs to comments. You can learn a lot from what your customers write in response to your posts.

- In your terms and conditions, give yourself the right to delete anything that abusive, but keep those which disagree with you because that opens up a helpful debate.

- Make your blogs useful and informative, and be sure that they represent your brand values.

78 LOGOS 2: THE SYMBOL

The word "brand" was first used to describe the mark made on cattle with a hot iron to identify the owner. But long before livestock were branded, makers would put their own mark on their products; the maker's mark has been used since at least Ancient Roman times.

In the 21st Century a brand is much more than a logo; some brands don't have them at all, but the logo is a visual symbol of a brand. That's why a good logo is memorable and distinctive. It saves customers time by helping them to find what they're looking for.

The idea

Nike's Swoosh is recognised worldwide.

As brand identity goes, it's far more successful than the name Nike, which gets pronounced in at least two different ways from the one the manufacturer uses. It rhymes with psyche and crikey, not like and bike, or Mickey and sticky. In Greek mythology Nike is the winged goddess who represents victory. They pronounce it Nikki.

In 1971 Phil Knight paid graphic designer Carolyn Davidson $35 for the logo. Later he did reward her more appropriately when the company became successful.

It looks like a tick, a mark of success, and fits well with their strapline "just do it". You can imagine a runner getting home from today's trip, ticking off the box on the to do list, feeling just the way the people at Nike hope she will.

It's a great logo because it's simple, easily recognised, will fit on clothes and sports equipment and it can be used forwards or backwards on the left and right sides of shoes.

In practice

- Shapes can be registered as trademarks so if you decide to use one, check first that it won't infringe someone else's property rights then register it as your own.
- Young companies, like Nike in 1971 and innocent drinks often get their friends in to draw a logo for them. If you've got friends with a sense of commercial design and some training at art college, by all means use their skills. Otherwise be clear about the brand values you want your logo to symbolise, and give the brief to a design agency.
- If you can make it work in one colour, it'll save a great deal in print costs.

79

LOGOS 3: LETTERING

There are font styles that have remained the same for over a hundred years, and are now so familiar that they've become neutral to the point of invisible. They are in millions of books and newspapers and on websites worldwide. We're too busy reading the words to notice their design.

There are others which are immediately associated with their own era. 50s, 60s and 70s fonts can bring an instant visual identity to a brand.

Some have been specially designed to grab our attention, when brands use their name, in their own original lettering, as their logo. They can be so distinctive that they're even recognisable when they're used to write a different brand name.

The idea

Coca-Cola has arguably the world's most recognisable lettering. Its flamboyant loops and waves make the words distinctive even when they are written in different alphabets from the original Roman, including Russian and Arabic.

Like other long-serving handwritten logos, such as Virgin, it's been very slightly tidied up, but has hardly changed since Coca Cola's book-keeper, Frank Mason Robinson designed it in the Spencerian handwriting script, which deserves a story of its own as it was Mr Spencer's attempt to give American handwriting a brand identity which he felt it lacked.

With its predominant colour, red, plus the distinctive bottle, the Coca-Cola handwriting consistently puts at the top of the list of the world's most recognisable brands.

In practice

- How catchy is your company name? You can make it into your logo by choosing a font that already exists, or by having one adapted or designed for you.
- Fonts themselves are covered by copyright so to use one as your own logo, you will probably have to license it from the designer. You can also commission your own and buy the rights.
- Use a design that is consistent with your brand personality. A law firm would probably avoid a 1950s US roadside diner font, unless they wanted to make a particular point.

80

WRITE THE BOOK

Even when you put a company history section on your website, there's never going to be room for the whole story. You'll also find that the information published about you online is never entirely accurate from your own point of view. And if you're not sufficiently well-known you can't even get yourself a Wikipedia entry. Tell your story yourself.

The idea

If you feel that your brand's story is interesting enough, you got tales to tell, secrets to share and wisdom to impart, write the book on paper or as a file customers can download.

Chefs and restaurants produce recipe books that introduce their brand identity to kitchens worldwide. Entrepreneurs write their autobiographies and even failed companies write up their tales of while, which we can read with a sense of schadenfreude, while hoping to learn from their mistakes.

In practice

- Can you write? Do you have the time? Lots of business books ghostwritten by professional authors or journalists, appointed by publishers or engaged by PR departments to do the job.
- Print or e-book? If you want this as a gift to present to your customers, or if your market is older than you probably want to

be on paper. But e-books are growing market and the electronic version will position your brand differently from print.

- The options for people wanting to be published these days are many and varied. If you have a publisher, you get a smaller share of the revenue but they take care of production, marketing and distribution. Self publishing, in print or electronically, gives you the control of the revenue but it's a lot of work, and you might not get access to the distribution channels you need.

81

FOLLOW YOUR NOSE

At school we learn that we have five senses, but actually we have many more. There's a sense of pain, acceleration, fear, proprioception (where our limbs are in relation to our torso), around 16 – 27 that scientists have identified at the time of writing, although there are disagreements about which ones are sufficiently independent of the others to be named.

The sense of smell is the most direct. Smell receptors leads straight into the oldest emotional part of the brain are the only ones with no protection from the air by skin or other membranes. That's why we can feel and emotion that a scent triggers before we can name what we are smelling. The part of the brain that recognises language developed later.

Smells trigger memories, good or bad, which is why companies like SLS Hotels aim to place good smells in nice places. Some organisations just smell the way they do, like biscuit factories, breweries and coffee roasters.

The idea

Lush shops, despite speculations to the contrary, do not pump their scent out onto the high street. But the company, who handmake their cosmetics using their own blends of essential oils and safe synthetics, use generous concentrations of perfumes in their fresh products. As they sell all their solid products unpackaged, the scent escapes of its own accord.

This means that whenever you're within a few hundred metres of a Lush shop, less when you're downwind of one, you can find it by following your nose. Like Marmite, you either love it or hate it, but the smell has certainly made its distinctive.

In practice

- If your brand has a scent, let it out. (But don't persecute people with it. Department store scent salespeople armed with atomisers can be terrifying.)
- Fragrance companies can create synthetic scents to match whatever atmosphere you wish to create, from new cars to barbecues to libraries.
- You can also commission and natural perfume made with plant essential oils and absolutes, which is a pleasantly environmentally friendly way to give your brand its own lovely smell.

82

QUESTION EVERYTHING

Doing the opposite of everyone else in your area of business is one way to position your brand differently, but you can shoot yourself in the foot. There's usually a good reason industries act the way they do; the ones who didn't might have lost their money, leaving others to carry on treading the usual path.

On the other hand, times change; new opportunities arise and the old rules can start to hold you back. It's worth taking a risk if you're certain you're right, and if you know it'll get you talked about by customers and the media.

The idea

Go to the fragrance department of any shop these days and there will be testers for you to try. The air is dense with fruity-floral smells, the scent of the moment, all mingled together like a thousand summer puddings next to a giant bunch of flowers. It's tricky to distinguish the one you want to try from what's already suspended in the air.

Take no notice of shop assistants offering you a bowl of coffee beans to sniff because this supposedly clears your sense of smell. It doesn't. It's another one of those rules that everyone in the industry follows simply because everyone in the industry follows it.

How do you make your scent brand stand out from a cloud of perfume?

Editions de Parfums Frederic Malle fill their shops with air that doesn't contain any perfume, not even their own. In some they have futuristic capsules that looked like a cross between Star Trek transporters and technologically advanced showers. In their Liberty of London boutique people have asked if they can use it to travel to the third floor. They're not for moving people, they're for moving air.

When you want to smell one of their fine fragrances, your sales assistant will blast the capsule full of fresh air, open the door and spraying your scent. You stick your head inside and inhale. This way, you get the impression of what you'll smell like when you're wearing it, the scent cloud you leave behind as you walk through room. It's what the French call the *sillage*, the wake, like the waves a boat leaves on a lake.

Their scents are expensive; they invite top perfumers to create their dream fragrances with no limit on the costs of ingredients. They want their customers to buy something they love, and to be certain they've chosen the right one. They definitely don't want anyone realising they bought the wrong thing once they get home.

In practice

- Ask yourself how your customers really experience your product or your service when they're in the outside world. How far can you go towards recreating that? Cars should be test driven in traffic jams, shoe shop should have areas with Tarmac, paving stones, grass and carpet.

- Go through your sales process and question all the points that you've never questioned before. Change the ones that turn out to be pointless.
- Tell the media what you've done. Invite the press and your customers to try it. The traditionalists might prefer the old way, but people soon adapt.
- PS If you need convincing that it's worth trying something completely new go to YouTube and search for "How to peel a banana like a monkey".

83 BRAND TONE OF VOICE

How does a brand put its values into a writing style? It defines its own tone of voice. Once you have identified what your brand stands for, and understood its personality, you can use language to represent it.

In any one language, we all pick from the same words but we can still sound very different. It's a bit like composers using the same instruments of the orchestra to create different moods.

The idea

One way to tell that an e-mail scam is a fake is to check the language. One claiming to be from the tax office turned up in my inbox recently announcing "You have a tax refund!!!" The UK Revenue Office is unlikely to use one exclamation mark, let alone three. An instant giveaway.

In recent years, large companies who write regularly to their customers have realised that their letters were being ignored because they were formed of long, impersonal sentences, industry jargon and pompous language. Instead of treating customers like people, they were just sending out the same old standard letters written for their own convenience not with the reader in mind.

Analysing their language to find gaps between the way they want to sound the customers and the way they have been coming across, helps organisations to develop new ways of writing which represents their brand values.

The danger is that you go too chummy, imitating another company's tone of voice instead of defining your own. Your language should support your brand identity not fight it. That's why the UK Revenue Office will never put three exclamation marks in their email subject line.

In practice

- Put yourself in your customers' shoes. Would you read to the end of your own letters? If they strike you as dull or patronising, it's time to change.
- Look closely at the language you're using. Does it match your brand's personality? It's not always easy to write in a different style, but there are companies who specialise in devising a new tone of voice and training people to use it.
- You can bring in creative business writers to help you redefine your tone of voice and train new and your people in the new skills they need to write in that way. You can always have brand language specialists rewrite your standard letters for you to help you get going.

84 BRAND EXTENSION

A brand with a good reputation is a useful thing. With a name that people trust and recognise you have a strong advantage over one that is starting from scratch.

Taking your company into a related area with new products or services used to be called brand stretching, but that sounded as if companies were trying too hard. So brand stretching rebranded itself. The new name is brand extension.

The idea

There are small steps a brand can take. Starbucks sell their instant coffee alongside their beans, or innocent drinks moving into selling single fruit juices. (Although innocent did rebrand their fruit waters, as Juicy Water.). Fashion brands known for their clothes often extend into developing accessories, and many of them license their brands to fragrance companies and venture into the potentially more profitable perfume industry.

In practice

- Look for a product or service that complements what you already do, so your customers will think that it's a natural extension of your brand, rather than raising their eyebrows in surprise.
- Let your existing customers know about your new venture.
- Make sure that the standards of your extended brand match those of your original, especially if it is being manufactured by a different organisation.

85 THE BISCUIT TEST

If your brand were a biscuit, what kind of biscuit would it be?

Does that seem like a silly question? Or perhaps you have tried it before and found that it works. Often your customers and your staff find it difficult to think of words to encapsulate what your brand stands for. But they might be able to identify your brand as Chocolate Hobnob, completely different from your competitor's brand, which they see as Custard Cream.

Using metaphors can help people define brand identity. People generally find it a lot easier to make comparisons than define concepts. So they can easily identify one brand as a Chocolate Hobnob, and another as a Custard Cream.

The idea

When your brand message doesn't seem to be making it through to your own staff or to your customers, one way to investigate this is to help people describe the way they see your brand. Often, the directors will have one vision of the brand, while the staff have a completely different idea. Customers will have their own ideas.

The biscuit test is a way to compare the differences. You can do the same exercise, asking what car would be closest to your brand, or which magazine, or dog. It can be a really helpful way to shed light on the differences between people's perceptions. Once you've identified the differences, you can find out what caused them, then work on your brand identity to minimise them.

In practice

- Once they've got over their scepticism, people usually find this exercise entertaining and will do their best to think of an accurate answer. It doesn't matter if they'd done it before.
- Even the sceptics will explain why they think it's silly, and give you the opportunity to find out what they think in different ways.
- A strong brand depends on the people inside having a similar view the people outside the organisation. Use the biscuit test to measure the gap, then use your discoveries to narrow it.

SEND CUSTOMERS AWAY EMPTY-HANDED

This is an exception, not a rule – you don't want to go out of business – but good brands are built on honesty. Give your customers a choice, and if you don't have what they need, send them to where they can get it.

There are brands with terrible reputations for hard selling; once they've got someone's attention they won't let go until they've made the sale, closed the deal and probably "upsold", talked the customer into buying more than they originally intended.

One problem salespeople have is that they're set short-term financial targets and are put under pressure to meet them. Their managers have their own targets and so the directors, each one expected to perform to standard. But if you push too hard when you're selling, you'll end up not only having customers warning their friends to stay away from you, they'll report you to the press, your industry watchdogs and Trading Standards.

The idea

Small businesses owners are personally responsible for their organisations' reputations and we can learn from the way they treat their customers.

One of the busiest little companies I know is PCS, a computer repair shop near my home. The first time I went there I asked to buy a new wireless router. Instead of asking me, "This one or that one?" Panos, the owner, asked me "What's not working?" Then he explained that if I tried a few things I'd probably be fine with the one I already owned. He was right since then I've been back for everything I need to keep my home office going.

Hermitage Oils' online store keeps an amazing range of rare perfumery materials. I ordered a basket full of obscure items like opoponax and goji berry absolutes for my personal perfume project. With my order confirmation, I also got an email from the owner, Adam Michael. He just wanted to warn me that the seaweed absolute I'd ordered was really difficult to work with and to check, before he took my money, that I was sure about it. I went ahead but I was grateful to him for pointing this out and it made me happy to shop there again.

In practice

- Individuals working for large organisations don't always think about their brands' reputations, but every relationship between one customer and one member of staff makes a difference. Your staff need to know that they are an important part of your organisation, and to understand their own part in influencing the way the outside world sees your brand.

- You can judge your financial targets and achievements in parallel with the Net Promoter Score, to measure the numbers of customers who go away unhappy.

- Think like a small business. If you were the owner and the personal relationships between the organisation and the customers were down to you, would you behave better?

TELL YOUR STORY

People like to know the real story behind the brand and about the people who work there. That's why the companies whose founders are still around to tell their own tales have a fascination that goes beyond what they are selling.

It's good to know that there was a Ben and Jerry. They sold up to Unilever, established by Lord Lever. Unilever's headquarters in the UK, the art deco building north west of Blackfriars Bridge, was Lord Lever's favourite hotel, so he bought it.

Pete & Johnny's Smoothies, which became PJ Smoothies, was bought by PepsiCo and disappeared in 2008. There was never a Pete or a Johnny.

The stories about your history show the human side of a brand. They also distinguish the fabricated brands from the genuine ones.

The idea

There's a usually space on a brand's website, often called About Us, where you can read about the founders and their history, look at old photographs and watch films about them. This is where an organisation can tell all the stories about their brand. Whether it started last week or 100 years ago, it's still interesting.

If there isn't one, then the brand lacks a sense of authenticity.

People are becoming more cynical and suspicious of marketing as a profession. If companies are going to keep their customer' trust, then it helps to show the real people running them. That men in suits who think of them as a demographic aren't trying to fool them. Unless you're in IT security, showing faces and telling stories remind customers that companies are made up of people too.

One of my favourites is the Pearl & Dean website, online home of the cinema advertising people. You can read about the two Mr Pearls and Mr Dean, but be warned that it plays their famous 1970s theme tune, which does rather smack you in the ears. There is a sweet story about how they met and started up the business, and a 1950s black and white photograph of them in evening dress with their wives in ball gowns.

Everyone who works for the business currently has their photograph on the website too, so if you call them you can picture you're speaking to.

In practice

- Tell the story of how your brand came into being and how you've been getting along since then. It will distinguish you from the invented ones.
- It's people who make a brand is what it is; knowing who they were and who they are now brings the brand values to life.
- Everyone within an organisation has a different version of their own brand story; each one is worth telling and listening to.

88 INNOVATION

Advertising agency joke.

How many creatives does it take to change a lightbulb?

Does it have to be a lightbulb?

Jim Stengel, left Procter & Gamble after working as their Global Marketing Officer, to set up his own consultancy. In his new book, he writes that it's people and innovation that are the two most important elements of successful brands.

Innovation, from the Latin for doing new stuff, means constantly thinking of bringing in new ways to do better, never deciding that what you've got is good enough, so you can sit back relax and watch it sell. Someone more innovative will overtake you.

Fortunately innovation is part of human nature.

The idea

Steve Zades runs an organisation called the Odyssey Network. As you can probably guess from the name, he takes people on voyages of discovery, although his aren't as dangerous as the original (and you don't have to kill anyone when you get home).

He organises journeys for business executives and creative teams to different countries, to experience cultural and commercial innovations outside their own industries.

He also creates innovation events, bringing creative minds from around the world to the same place to share ideas. Steve believes in a new ROI, return on innovation, and that it's a brand's innovation strategy that will keep it going and growing.

In practice

- Give 20% of your resources to innovation. That's one day of the working week for everyone.
- New ideas have got to come from somewhere, and it's not usually from sitting at your desk looking at Google. Get yourself and your people out and about.
- Ideas can come from watching contemporary dance, walking the dog or learning Japanese. If you restrict yourself to your own industry, it puts boundaries on your innovation. Take time for new experiences, and you'll find ideas you never knew you were looking for.

89 | CREATIVE PARTNERSHIPS

Partnerships between two brands can create something magical. In a joint creative venture, what can be produced should be something even better than what the two sides can create separately.

The idea

Liberty is a beautiful London department store; it was opened in 1875, and the current shop was built in the 1920s, in Tudor revival style (known less kindly as mock-Tudor by the Modernists), from the timbers of two decommissioned battleships.

Sir Arthur Lasenby Liberty brought beautiful, exotic items from all around the world and commissioned the designers of the day to create household goods for sale in his store. Liberty continues his tradition in the 21st-century.

Liberty collaborates with a surprising range of brands. In 2011, they created a bestselling range of Liberty print trainers with Nike. The Liberty print FitFlops sold out too. Liberty and the US company Target worked together to make a modern, affordable range in Liberty prints. With Apple, Liberty created covers for products including iPhones, iPads and MacBooks. Then there's the Miller Harris Liberty fragrance, Rose en Noir, and Paris retailer Merci's suitcases in floral Liberty prints.

Liberty actively search for interesting brands to collaborate with; they can be huge, they can be small. What's crucial is that their brand values mesh to create something stronger: Products that are useful and beautiful that wouldn't have come into being on their own.

In practice

- Seek out brands with similar values to yours, people you would love to work with.
- If both sides bring creativity to the project, all the better; be prepared for strong opinions.
- Limited editions always have the catch-them-now-or-they're-gone-forever extra added charm, and also attract interest from the press.Work with organisations that share similar brand values.

SPOT THE CELEBRITY

When someone famous chooses your brand, you can tell the press or you can choose to keep quiet. It depends on the person. Some famous people go out looking for publicity, and others are happy to get on with their lives quietly without much fuss. We see one of the "Strictly Come Dancing" stars at our local butcher's shop, but no-one kicks up a stir about it. There's an Oscar winning actor who goes to our Waitrose, but they don't take his picture and send it to the gossip mags.

On the other hand, celebrities – people who make a career out of being famous for being famous – often expect to get their shopping for nothing in exchange for press coverage, on the grounds that their admirers will want what they want, and will come in to buy it. They consider their recommendation to be good enough to increase sales, and sometimes it is. The Duchess of Cambridge can sell out a dress in a day, but she does pay her own way.

The idea

Magazines which feature the lives of the rich and famous are always looking for stories about celebrities, so press offices will give them information to help them fill their columns in exchange for a mention of the brand.

It's a good way of getting into the media, as long as you're happy to be associated with the celebrities concerned. Many shops don't court the celeb circuit, but they're delighted when someone famous turns up and buys something of their own accord. But they'll immediately send out a press release with the list of everything on the shopping list.

You risk driving famous people away if they know they are going to be used to sell your products. Some prefer to be able to shop in peace and to be treated with discretion.

On the other hand, there are celebs available for hire through their agents. They will show up at press launches for a fee, so you can take photographs of them with your brand and send them to the gossip columns. Decide whether or not this would help or hinder your brand values. Some brand owners get stars in their eyes and make the wrong decision.

In practice

- If you're fortunate enough to have a famous customer, you could use the publicity to attract people who admire their style, but if you want to keep their business it would be better to ask their permission first. It all depends whether you rather have them recommend their friends, or attract their fans.

- You might be able to come to a reasonable arrangement where you give a discount or free products in exchange for associating them with your brand name. Unless you are a charitable organisation or a social enterprise, you'll probably have to pay for the privilege of featuring famous people in your publicity.

- If you align your brand with a celebrity, choose carefully; like everyone else, they can be unpredictable.

91 BRAND GUIDELINES

You've gone to the trouble and expense of having your logo designed, your fonts agreed and your written tone of voice defined. Maybe you've had your ambient perfume commissioned, decided on your strapline, and chosen the exact Pantone reference for your two corporate colours. You need the whole organisation to use them the right way in the right places.

The idea

People are inventive. They love to add their own decorative touches and interpretations. What they don't always consider is that each time they alter your carefully thought out brand identity, they make customers less likely to recognise it.

If you make this clear to your staff, and give them guidelines to follow, then they've got the toolkit in place. Everyone can work together to make your brand more recognisable, not less.

There's a very big communications technology brand that produced its brand guidelines as a lovely hardback coffee table book and leaves it out for customers to see – which is great. When it comes to the writing, it has a couple of pages explaining how their brand values should be encapsulated in the written tone of voice, which is to be friendly, human and chatty. Then it gives a page of examples of befores and afters, but it doesn't give the staff the skills to change their own writing.

In practice

- As well as the what and the why, you need the how. Show your people how to use the guidelines correctly.

- Provide templates and standard formats for design and writing. Make them easily accessible on your intranet. Even better, give people training so that they learn how to produce their own.

- Include what not to do, or someone will give it a try.

92 BEWARE THE BRAND'S EVIL TWIN

As soon as your brand becomes successful, chances are it will be copied. There are shopping malls in the Far East which are entirely fully of counterfeit brands with their own almost exact copies of the genuine brands' shops. If someone can find a way to do what you do but cheaper,and take advantage of the work you've put into building your own brand identity, then they will.

If it's any consolation, it only happens once you're successful enough to attract their attention, but it's irritating, it's expensive to defend your intellectual property legally and it can damage your business.

The issue of counterfeiting is a complicated one but the shadow industry exists because people want a bargain, and they are prepared to convince themselves that anything with your logo on it has as much value as the real thing, even if it's obviously not as well manufactured.

The idea

It's not just the Far East, although China is the world's biggest source of counterfeits. Every country in the world makes fakes; the UK specialises in counterfeit – poisonous – vodka. Others fake prescription drugs. Wherever there are high prices and high demand, someone will produce the rip-off version.

It can be top brands fighting each other. The unseemly scrap between YSL and Louboutin over red shoe soles is an obvious challenge to Louboutin's brand positioning, but IP law hasn't helped him.

It can be the big guys going for the small guys. One huge UK clothing retailer was notorious for taking small designers' ideas, mass producing them more cheaply, then, when the small companies complained, perhaps hoping for some financial recognition of their contribution to profits, they'd get a letter back saying (in legal language), "Oh dear. We're sorry about that, we didn't realise. We've withdrawn the line." In the meantime they've ruined the market for the original designers and cost them the legal fees too.

Usually, those big companies whose strategy is to take "inspiration" from wherever they can get it, without having to pay for it, are careful enough to make the copy obvious to the customer, but sufficiently different to escape legal problems. That doesn't make it right though, and it's something that small, dynamic, creative brands constantly come up against, and sometimes they become so disillusioned that they give up entirely. At least you can trace the big companies' sources.

The illegal counterfeiters are often impossible to find, let alone sue. It's the role of Trading Standards to find them, seize their merchandise and prosecute them.

In practice

- Register your trademarks (paid for) and defend your copyright (free). Read up on intellectual property law on the government's IP law website, and consult an IP lawyer if you need to. Sometimes it is as simple as sending a legal letter to point out that your intellectual property is being infringed and to ask them to stop.
- Be aware. Ask your customers to help you find copies and counterfeits, and report them to Trading Standards, whether they turn up on market stalls or in supermarkets.
- Have your own intellectual property strategy in place, and a lawyer ready to act. Decide who's worth pursuing in court and who isn't. Never do it on a point of principle if it's going to cost you a lot of money you could use to develop new ideas.

93 ENTREPRENEURIAL BRANDS

In times of economic growth, conditions are perfect for the entrepreneurial brand. There is a classic business school method of brand building, which aims to make a lot of money in a very short time for its owner and developer by selling to a large, established company. There are benefits to both sides. The big company doesn't have to take the risk of developing its own brand; the initial investors make their fortunes. Sometimes.

The idea

You study for your MBA and you learn the rules of how to create a cool brand in a short space of time. You develop your business plan, take it to venture capital companies (VCs) for funding, put the plan into action, attract the attention of corporations in your market, then sell out.

The VC gets its investment back with a big financial return, the corporation gets a new brand without having to do all the investment in creativity and the brand owner tuckers his or her millions safely away in the bank ready to start again, or retire for ever, or become a venture capitalist.

VCs expect a very high return on their investment, because they often lose their money when brands crash and burn before they are bought. If they don't get a big corporate buyer, these brands rarely break even because their debts are too high.

The LV logo has appeared in different colours and in designs alongside Murakami's smiling daisies and cherries, but has never been dropped from his range of canvas luggage.

When a logo has used initials for over 100 years, and is a widely recognised part of the brand, ignore the trends and keep using it.

In practice

- Be prepared that if you shorten your company name to its initials, then people will start to call it by the short form.
- Initials might be short and snappy, but they might be confused with someone else's brand. Use your own name if your initials are too generic as a brand name.
- If you've been using your initials as your brand and your logo for longer than anyone remembers, like IBM, JCB and NCR, keep them.

STRAPLINES

A strapline is the thing you say about yourself that you put under the brand name or at the bottom of every page. It's a very short statement of what you do or what your brand stands for.

Do you need one? Not always. They do help customers to understand what your brand is all about, so if in doubt, try it.

The idea

There are straplines that aim to persuade you to buy, those which give you an image of how wonderful it's to use their brand, amusing ones, those which try to make you feel better about yourself for buying into their vision, and some great ones which have been banned for not being justifiable, including "Guinness is good for you", "A Mars a day helps you work, rest and play" and "Winston tastes good like a cigarette should".

At the time, the Winston line caused more of a stir at the ungrammatical use of "like" instead of "as" than any question about using the word "good" in the same sentence as "cigarette".

There are websites that will help you generate your own strapline. For my writing company, Slogaizer.net came up with "Feel good with Little Max", "Little Max, in touch with tomorrow" and "Little Max never lies". It's easy to write bad ones that have no relevance to your brand at all. It's harder to come up with something short that illuminates your purpose.

Your strapline should be true and justifiable, and within the

Advertising Standards Authority's (ASA) guidelines, or impossible to disprove, like BMW's strapline: The Ultimate Driving Machine.

Some are intriguingly evocative like the Spanish shoe company, Camper, with the strapline "Walk, don't run" or Muji's "no-brand goods".

In practice

- Check on the ASA website what you can legally say about your brand in your publicity online and off, and with Trading Standards about packaging. Their UK sites are www.asa.org.uk and www.tradingstandards.gov.uk.
- Get your most creative minds together and write a long list of possible straplines, cut it down to a shortlist, think about it for a couple of weeks and go with the one you prefer.
- If you don't want one, don't have one. Some huge brands don't bother because they don't feel the need to explain themselves any further.

BE THE GENERIC

Sometimes your brand name will turn into a verb, and sometimes it's going to be a noun. Occasionally a brand turns into a metaphor, as in the case of "doing a Ratner", saying something so disastrous about your company that you eventually cause its failure.

Verb brands: To Hoover, to Google, to Skype, to Fedex, to Photoshop, to Sellotape.

Noun brands: Rollerblade is used for in-line skate, Kleenex is used in the US for paper tissue or paper hankie, Perrier is used for sparkling water. Even Heroine was a brand name in the days when it was legal to buy opium over the counter in the form of the medicine, laudanum.

The most widely used is probably the Biro, the balloint pen invented by László Biró. It was licensed by the British Royal Air Force for using at high altitude, then sold to Marcel Bich's company in 1950 for his Bic pen company in France. Biró himself called his pen the Birome.

The idea

If you're the first in the market, or the one that does the most advertising to get your brand name known, you're in a position to become the generic. At the moment, there's a brand called Sugru, a strong synthetic putty that sets hard to repair things. It's set to become a generic because those of us who use it find it a lot easier to call it that than, "the synthetic putty that sets hard". There isn't anything else like it so they can create their own new word for it.

In Perrier's case it works for them. If someone asks for a Perrier, they'll be brought a Perrier unless the restaurant doesn't stock it, at which point your waiter will tell you which brands you can have. People realise that it's the brand name, but use it to mean sparkling water.

In Rollerblade's case, they aren't as happy about it. Unless you're a keen skater, you probably think that an inline skate is really called a roller blade. Becoming the generic name for something can be a help, or a hindrance.

In practice

- You can't always control whether or not this will happen to your brand.
- If you're the ground-breaker in a new market, then your brand name could be adopted as the generic. Use it as a verb on all your publicity material.

97 THE TAG

In the 80s brands started to put labels on the outside of their clothing, partly to make their brand better known, and partly because it became cool to show off what you were wearing among certain groups. What you wear and how you wear is strongly influenced by your social group. People who denounce the vulgarity of being seen with your labels showing probably belong to a group of people who feel the same way, and vice versa.

In some countries it's the done thing to leave on the lightly stitched label that suit manufacturers put on the sleeve so shop assistants can find them easily amongst the rails of other dark coloured suits. (I once mistakenly pointed out to a chap that he had accidentally left his label on. He thought I was a complete idiot. Why would he take off a label that told the world he had bought a Dior suit?)

In China, women leave the price tags on their Louis Vuitton handbags to show that they've paid full price for the real thing, rather than buying a counterfeit. Naturally, the counterfeiters responded by adding fake price tags, and will even supply you with a fake receipt.

This is one part of branding that appears to have taken leave of its senses, the part that guided London's rioters and looters to smash windows and steal brands that were cool among their social group, and completely ignore silver jewellery or expensive gifts that didn't have the right label on them. But the brand owners must be doing something right because if people will go to the trouble of stealing your goods, at least it proves that they're desirable.

The idea

There are ways of saying, "this is one of ours" without broadcasting your brand identity to the watching world. It's halfway between being anonymous and putting a huge logo on everything you do.

One of the earliest was Steiff's "Knopf im Ohr", now translated for the international market: "Button in Ear". The German company distinguished its toys by putting a little stud, with an elephant on it, into each the ear of each toy. The elephant was the first toy that the company's founder made. They now have a less subtle golden stud, with the Steiff name, not the elephant, and a yellow ribbon so you can't miss it. They've been doing this since 1904 so that people could recognise the Steiff brand and the quality that came with the button. The first bears that were made now sell for tens of thousands of pounds and the first thing that experts look for is the stud.

Radley bags all have a Scottie dog mark on them, either as a metal stud on the luggage, or as a leather tag, in a contrasting colour to the main bag. Second hand Radley bags retain their value on eBay, as long as they still have the dog tag with them.

Kickers boots and shoes have little daisy-shaped tags. When children wear out their old ones, they keep the tags and add them to the new shoes.

Paul Smith's smart grey briefcases have a luggage tag in his signature striped leather. His shirts have different coloured buttonhole embroidery. His canvas shoes have one brightly coloured eyelet for the laces.

Mont Blanc pens have a snow-capped pen top.

These are details for people who already know the brand; they are for people who are quite happy for others to recognise their belongings, but don't want to be used as an advertising medium.

In practice

- People like quirky. If you can find an original way to identify your products, and you can also trademark it, you can walk the path between anonymous and overt.
- Here we're talking about something other than a logo; it's an extra bonus, something that other brands haven't thought of or would find too much of a bother.
- This is branding for introverts; people who like to please themselves and aren't that bothered about making a big statement.

98 ADD A SOFA

Coffee and tea shops have tables and chairs. When you have finished your coffee, you leave. Some have waitresses who come to the table to place your order. Self-service cafeterias have counters. Coffee was often instant, or it was made with a machine that gurgled weakly. And suddenly a coffeehouse with sofas opened.

The idea

Starbucks is successful because it was a hundred thousand percent better than the archaic, badly run, rudely staffed cafes we'd been stuck with. Yes, there were some good ones; many of them are still there and doing nicely because Starbucks made going out for a coffee into a leisure activity, so they pulled their socks up, tried harder and joined in. Near me, one coffee shop owner was desperate to retire but couldn't find anyone to buy the business. When Starbucks moved next door, they didn't lose all their customers and fail, they got busier and sold to Costa Coffee for enough to retire comfortably.

They created a space for specialist organic and single estate coffees bean companies to set up and thrive; they have FairTrade coffees; most of all they give you somewhere to go and sit in a comfortable chair, and don't give you the evil eye if you stay to do your emails after you've finished your drink.

In practice

- What do people really want? When they find a brand that gives it to them, they flock there.
- Make your customers feel welcome.
- Often we don't realise we're accepting low standards as normal until someone comes along with an alternative. Then it seems so obvious that we slap our foreheads and wonder why we didn't think of it ourselves. So what would make a huge difference in your area of businesses? How about giving it a go with your brand?

SUPPORT YOUR CAUSE

There are people who think that organic farming, fair trade for developing countries, banning animal testing, reducing landfill and lowering carbon emissions are passing fads which can be incorporated into their marketing strategy until it's more fashionable to support a new cause. For others it's their life's work.

The idea

There are organisations, foundations and associations whose role is to encourage customers to buy ethical products, from Fair Trade chocolate to vegan cosmetics, organic cotton clothes to unpackaged vegetables.

They are funded by their partner organisations, who pay for the following: to have their products scrutinised, for advice on how to get them up to standard, and for the right to put the certification mark on their own packaging.

The idea is that the mark will help to distinguish a brand from the others who aren't certified, and that this will encourage customers to buy it. Even if people don't normally seek out organic or fairly traded goods, when there is a choice, they prefer to have the good feeling that they are helping out in a small way when they buy the certified product.

No-one would buy Divine chocolate just because it's got Fairtrade certification, and 45% of the company is owned by their cocoa producer, Kuapa Kokoo. It just happens to be one of the tastiest chocolates on the planet (in my view) and it's very good value.

Kuapa Kokoo is a co-operative based in Ghana. They were already selling their cocoa butter to Europe, and they had Fairtrade status. They formed the Day Chocolate Company in 1998 with Twin Trading and The Body Shop, with the support of Comic Relief and Christian Aid, named in memory of Richard Day from the Twin Trading team. In 2007, they changed their name to Divine Chocolate Ltd, a brand which is self-explanatory when you've tasted it.

They pay for certification and carry the Fairtrade mark on their chocolate packaging, so as well as sharing their recognisable logo, they are also promoted during Fairtrade Fortnight. The Fairtrade site at fairtrade.org.uk lists all the producs with their certification on sale in the UK.

In practice

- Products and ingredients can be traded fairly, or organic or cruelty free without having certification, but they don't get the logo on their goods, or the publicity that goes with it. The more partners the associations have, the stronger their own brands will become.
- If you feel strongly about an issue, you probably already know the organisation that deals with certification. Joining will help to bring the issue to a wider audience.
- To campaign in other areas, you can align your brand with a charity or social enterprise and work in partnership with them.

DO SOMETHING OUTRAGEOUS

It's not as easy as it used to be to get into the Guinness Book of Records; they've banned all the silly things that might hurt people. But it's not impossible. There are other things that get you noticed, as well as record breaking.

It's got to be something that would make people think, "Wow, fancy doing that!" and not "Blimey, that was stupid."

The idea

Sir Richard Branson has carried out a series of publicity generating events. He raced across the Atlantic ocean in his speedboat, the Virgin Atlantic Challenger, to win the Blue Riband speed record in 1986. He and Per Lindstrand were the first people to cross the Atlantic in a hot air balloon.

When he got old enough to pick up his bus pass, he scaled down his adventures a little and has had a couple of disasters, such as crashing into a wall while abseiling down a hotel building and tipping himself and his beautiful passenger off a jet ski into a Las Vegas lake. He also had to abandon his 2008 Atlantic crossing in a yacht named Virgin Money, at about the same time as when the recession kicked in.

The story of one of the most outrageous acts was made into a film, Calendar Girls, and changed the image of the Women's Institute forever. One Yorkshire branch of the WI modelled for their own calendar, naked except for strategically placed tea, cakes and flower arrangements, to raise money for leukaemia research.

Lush once held the record for the world's largest soap.

In practice

- Make it a team effort, rather than a solo performance. Get your people involved. That way, even if it goes pear-shaped it will have been good to take part.
- Choose something that will fit beautifully with your brand values. It doesn't have to be dangerous. If you aren't an outrageous organisation, you could organise a knitting festival, or the world's largest yoga class. It doesn't have to break a record, just get noticed.
- Raising funds for a good cause at the same time will help to get media coverage, at the same time as doing something positive.